HARNESSING THE FLOW OF THE UNIVERSE

Samuel Ebeid

DEDICATION

To my beloved wife, Karen Ebeid,

This book is dedicated to you, my greatest inspiration. Your unwavering support and boundless love have shaped both this book and my life. May this book serve as a testament to our love and strength, a reminder of our remarkable journey together.

With love,
Samuel Ebeid

Table of Contents

INTRODUCTION

Have you ever wondered about the true nature of the universe and your place within it? Have you felt a desire to tap into a higher power and become the master of your own reality? If so, then this book, "Harnessing the Flow of the Universe," is your guide to unlocking the limitless potential that resides within you.

With heartfelt excitement, I extend a warm welcome to you, dear reader, as we embark together on this overpowering journey. This work is not just a collection of words on paper; rather, it is a transformative journey that beckons us to unlock the extraordinary power living within the depths of our being. Within the upcoming pages, I humbly share a mantra that has served and is still serving as an unwavering compass in my own journey, shaping my reality, and pouring within me a profound sense of happiness and well-being.

Beyond the role of an author, I am a fellow traveler on this path, eager to share the insights, tools, and wisdom that have illuminated my own path. Through the exploration of this mantra, my goal is not only to enhance your understanding of its power but to encourage you to create and develop your own mantra, reciting it regularly to achieve mastery on your journey of harnessing the flow of the universe.

In this book, I'm sharing profound insights about harnessing the universe's flow. While it might seem like I've figured it all out, the truth is, this work is a guide for both you and me—a humble seeker on an ongoing journey of discovery. As I share my knowledge and experiences, I believe there's always more to learn and deeper powers to discover.

This isn't a claim of mastery but a shared exploration, a journey to unlock the greatest secrets and powers. Together, we navigate possibilities, learning, and growth, recognizing that the journey itself is the key to understanding and potential. Let's embark on this expedition as companions, contributing our unique experiences to harnessing the universe's extraordinary flow.

As we navigate through the chapters ahead, envision this book as a lantern illuminating the shadows of uncertainty, offering you the means to navigate the details of your own unique journey. It is my sincere hope that you find inspiration, guidance, and a transformative power within these pages, pushing you toward a future where you are the master of your destiny. So, let the exploration commence, and may the wisdom unveiled within these words guide you towards a life abundant with fulfillment, purpose, and the harmonious dance with the flow of the universe.

*

As previously noted, this book is a study of my personal mantra—a creation and development that has progressed over the past few years. Reciting this mantra regularly, I see it as a guiding beacon harmonizing with the rhythm of my life. It has pushed me toward realms of joy, abundance, and self-realization, becoming an essential part of my journey.

In these pages, I share the essence and transformative power of this mantra, hoping it resonates with you as it has with me, illuminating your path toward a life filled with contentment and purposefulness.

Now, let me introduce the mantra that serves as a central focus throughout this book. In the chapters to follow, we will systematically break down each part, investigating into detailed discussions to illuminate the profound knowledge embedded within. Without further ado, here is the mantra in its entirety, laying the foundation for our exploration and understanding in the chapters ahead.

∗∗∗

"Hi, my name is Sam, and now I'm so HAPPY and feel so GOOD, because of how far I've come in my life and because of all the great things coming my way right now. I'm blessed, appreciative, grateful, and thankful for everything I have, all I had, all the experiences I went through, and everything I'm going through right now. And I know, like I know, like I know with unwavering faith that all this is happening for a reason, a good reason, actually it's a great reason. It's just the universe responding to the nature of my soul, to the song of my heart, and to my prayers. And I know, like I know, like I know with unwavering faith that the universe is rearranging itself for me right now to give me exactly what I want. And what I want is: ...., ..., ..., ..., ... And I know, like I know, like I know with unwavering faith that this is all happening for me right now, and that I'm pulling off a miracle, the miracle of harnessing the flow of the universe. Amen and thank you."

***

Before we embark on the chapters that lie ahead, it's important to acknowledge that I intentionally didn't present my personal list of desires to the universe when I shared my own mantra with you. The deliberate omission serves as a foundation to a vital revelation awaiting us in the following pages.

As we delve into the details of crafting and developing our individual mantras, we'll discover the empowering ability to list and modify our wishes at will, forming them into personalized expressions that align seamlessly with our unique aspirations and desires. This intentional omission invites you to embrace the flexibility and personalization characteristic in the mantra creation process, as we discover the transformative potential of tailoring our own affirmations to initiate the manifestation of our dreams.

***

As we board on this journey through the following chapters, we will breakdown the aspects of this mantra, transforming it into an arsenal of powerful tools. Each chapter unfolds as a steppingstone, guiding us with precision and purpose on the path to mastering the profound art of harnessing the flow of the universe.

In Chapter One, the focus is on the art of living in the moment, an investigation that extends beyond the acknowledgment of the present. We dig deep into the core of the now, embracing it with open hearts and receptive minds. This chapter becomes a beacon, inviting us to harmonize our existence with the rhythmic pulse of the universe, fostering a sharp awareness that becomes the foundation for the transformative journey ahead.

As we progress to Chapter Two, the spotlight turns to the powerful impact of cultivating a consistent state of joy and happiness while reciting the mantra. This exploration isn't merely about feeling good; it's a profound inquiry into the vibrational frequencies we release into the cosmos. The mantra becomes a channel for positive energy, inviting us to celebrate the quality of happiness and, in turn, attracting similar energies from the universe.

Chapter Three ushers us into the transformative realm of gratitude. Within the framework of the mantra, gratitude emerges not merely as a momentary emotion but as a dynamic force capable of unlocking the gates to an abundance of positivity. We explore the profound interconnection between expressing gratitude and the ability to attract more blessings into our lives. In this chapter, the mantra transforms into a tool that opens the floodgates of appreciation, creating a magnetic field that draws in the goodness that the universe has to offer.

In essence, these chapters collectively form a comprehensive guide, unlocking the multi-layered potential within the mantra. As we navigate through these teachings, envision each chapter as a key that unlocks a new dimension of understanding and application. Together, we will untie the complexities of this transformative journey, progressively refining our ability to harness the flow of the universe and become designers of our own realities.

Chapter Four is a deep dive into the realm of affirmation, exploring how deliberate and positive declarations, when woven into the fabric of the mantra, become catalysts for reshaping our subconscious mind. This chapter is a profound exploration of the power of intentional language, as affirmations seamlessly integrate into the mantra, amplifying its transformative influence.

In Chapter Five, the spotlight is on belief—a cornerstone in the foundation of manifesting desires. We unravel the effectiveness of unwavering faith, understanding how cultivating a firm belief in the mantra's affirmations enhances its effectiveness. As the mantra becomes an instrument of belief, it transforms from a series of words into a dynamic force shaping the trajectory of our reality.

In Chapter six, we explore how the universe responds to our alignment and mastery of the tools discussed in earlier chapters. As we attune ourselves to its flow, we uncover the intriguing interplay between our intentional actions and cosmic forces, delving into the profound dance of cause and effect in our existence.

The following chapters continue the journey, each unlocking a unique facet of the transformative process. Chapter Seven delves into the art of asking, where the mantra becomes a channel for expressing our desires to the universe. Visualization takes center stage in Chapter Eight, exploring the vivid imagery that aligns our intentions with the cosmic flow, creating a vivid blueprint for the life we wish to manifest.

Chapter Nine explores the crucial element of certainty required to make the mantra effective in aligning ourselves with the flow of the universe. As we explore the final component of unwavering faith that concludes the mantra, we unlock the key to its effectiveness. The chapter unravels the significance of certainty in our beliefs and how it acts as a powerful catalyst in manifesting the desired alignment with the cosmic forces.

After finishing the study of the mantra, Chapter Ten comes to delve into the profound significance of controlling our thoughts and words beyond the scope of the mantra. Here, we explore the extensive influence of our inner dialogue and the words we choose, emphasizing their profound impact on our ability to harness the universe's flow. This chapter acts as a pivotal guide to cultivating a mindset aligned with the vibrational frequencies necessary for manifesting our deepest desires.

In closing of this book, let this be an earnest invitation—a whispered promise that echoes through the pages of this transformative journey. As we conclude our study of harnessing the flow of the universe, let us not merely part ways but linger a moment longer in the realm of profound inspiration.

So, let's carry this invitation in our heart as we navigate the currents of life. May it be a constant reminder that, in embracing hope, strength, laughter, play, living in the moment, smiling often, dreaming big, and choosing happiness, we become the maestro of our own symphony, orchestrating a life that resonates with the harmonious flow of the universe.

***

Now, are you prepared to take the first step into the wondrous journey of harnessing the fascinating flow of the universe? The path we are about to tread is nothing short of miraculous, a transformative journey that invites us to unlock the hidden possible within and wield the extraordinary power that resides at the intersection of intention and cosmic energies. Together, let's explore this mystical realm, where each revelation is a steppingstone towards personal empowerment and a profound connection with the forces that shape our reality. It's a journey that promises to unravel the mysteries of your own existence and unveil the boundless wonders that await us in the uncharted territories of self-discovery. So, with anticipation in our hearts and courage in our spirits, let's take the dive and witness the magic that unfolds when we align with the flow of the universe.

1 LIVING IN THE MOMENT

In our journey to unlock the secrets of this universe's symphony, we delve into the first chapter, where we are confronted with a fundamental truth – that one of the keys to harnessing the flow of the universe lies in our ability to embrace the present. This chapter unveils the initial tools essential for navigating the currents of cosmic energy that shape our reality.

Living in the moment is not a plain concept; it is a deliberate and transformative practice that fills our daily lives. In this chapter, we examine the details of this art, understanding how it forms the foundation for our journey toward mastering the flow of the universe. The emphasis here is on the profound impact of living in the moment, particularly during the simple yet powerful acts of reading and reciting our mantra.

In our exploration, we learn to liberate ourselves from the shackles of the past and the anxieties of the future. By engaging ourselves in the current moment, especially when engaged in the sacred practice of reciting our mantra, we align our heart with the harmonious vibrations of the universe. This alignment is not just a philosophical concept; it is a tangible connection that deepens with each intentional breath.

The pages ahead unfold a narrative of discovery, encouraging a shift in perspective and the cultivation of a heightened awareness. As we embrace the present, we pave the way for a transformative journey, one that aligns us with the rhythmic pulse of the universe. Join us on this exploration of "The Art of Living the Moment," where the wisdom of the cosmos beckons us to dance with the present, forging a connection that transcends the boundaries of time and space.

***

The initial self-introduction:

Now, let's delve deeper into the relationship between living in the moment and the creation and development of our mantra. In my own mantra introduced at the beginning of this book, we can observe that a personalized and intimate expression of self could serves as a powerful channel for establishing a profound connection with the universe.

The initial self-introduction, "Hi, my name is Sam," is not just a routine gesture; it is a ceremonial greeting to the cosmos. As we extend this salutation, it becomes a gateway for meaningful dialogue with the universe. In this interaction, we lay our deepest thoughts, desires, and vulnerabilities, approaching the cosmic realm with open hearts and eager spirits. This self-disclosure is not just a formality but an intentional act that sets the stage for a sacred exchange.

Within this dialogue, we bring our entire spectrum of human experience—our hopes, dreams, fears, and aspirations—into the cosmic conversation. It is a genuine sharing of our essence, fostering a sense of trust and openness in our spiritual practice. The universe becomes not just an observer but a participant in our journey, an active listener to the melody of our aspirations.

Moving to the second part of the mantra, we find a crucial element that ties seamlessly into the practice of living in the moment—acknowledging our present emotions. Reciting a part of the mantra like: "and now I'm so happy and feel so good " becomes more than a declaration; it is a conscious recognition of our emotional state in the current moment. This acknowledgment is a pivotal aspect of the art of living in the moment.

By recognizing and articulating our current emotions, we create a bridge between our internal landscape and the vast cosmic expanse. The emphasis on genuine present feeling in our mantra is a powerful proclamation that resonates with the universe. In this declaration, we affirm that we are filled with happiness and a profound sense of well-being, choosing to embrace these positive emotions wholeheartedly in the present time.

This act of genuine and current feeling is not a superficial expression but a deliberate effort to tap into the transformative power of emotions. Even amid challenges and uncertainties, we consciously cultivate joy and positivity. We understand that this emotional resonance is the key that unlocks the doors of manifestation and transformation in the cosmic dance of the universe.

In essence, the mantra becomes more than words; it transforms into a dynamic expression of our existence in the present moment. Through this intentional practice, we weave a connection with the universe, embracing the now with authenticity, vulnerability, and a profound awareness of the emotional currents that shape our reality. The mantra becomes a living testament to our journey, a rhythmic heartbeat that harmonizes with the cosmic pulse, guiding us towards a deeper understanding of the art of living in the moment.

***

Living in the Present in the Mantra:

In our journey of crafting, developing, and reciting our mantras on a regular basis, a vital piece of advice emerges as a guiding beacon – the deliberate and intentional practice of living in the moment. It is through this conscious immersion into the present that we can forge a deeper and more profound connection with the universe, transforming our mantra and the act of living in the moment into powerful tools for harnessing the mysterious flow of the cosmic currents.

As we embark on the creation and development of our personal mantras, the process extends beyond the mere construction of words. It transcends the boundaries of linguistic expression and becomes a sacred act of co-creation with the universe. The mantra, an intimate reflection of our aspirations and deepest desires, is not just a sequence of syllables but a vibrational resonance that echoes through the cosmos.

To enhance the efficacy of our mantra, we must intentionally infuse the practice with a heightened awareness of the present moment. This means not merely reciting the words mechanically but immersing ourselves fully in the now, savoring each breath, and relishing the profound experience of the present. It is a deliberate choice to be fully present, to let go of the shackles of past regrets and future anxieties, and to embrace the current moment as the only reality.

Living in the moment becomes the vessel in which the transformation of connection occurs. As we recite our mantra, the act of living in the present serves as a magnifying glass, intensifying the resonance of our intentions with the vibrational frequencies of the universe. In these moments of deliberate presence, our mantra transforms into a dynamic force, a channel through which our desires and energies seamlessly merge with the cosmic flow.

The universe, in its vast and complicated dance, responds to the sincerity and authenticity of our engagement with the present. The more we consciously live the moment during mantra recitation, the stronger the connection we cultivate with the rhythmic pulse of the cosmos. It becomes a reciprocal exchange, a sacred dialogue where our intentions are met with the responsive energies of the universe, creating a harmonious dance that transcends the limitations of individual existence.

This intentional living in the moment is not a momentary practice; it becomes a way of being, a lifestyle that fills every aspect of our daily existence. As we link the art of living in the present with the regular recitation of our mantra and beyond, we unlock the potential for transformation on a grand scale. The mantra, infused with the essence of the present moment, becomes a resonant frequency that tunes our consciousness to the universal wavelength, facilitating the harnessing of the flow of the universe.

In conclusion, the advice resonates as a call to not merely utter our mantras but to infuse them with the spirit of the present. It beckons us to live the moment consciously and deliberately during our mantra recitation, transforming these moments into sacred portals through which we establish a profound connection with the universe. In making the mantra and living in the present vital aspects of our spiritual practice, we wield powerful tools that harmonize our existence with the cosmic currents, paving the way for a transformative journey of harnessing the majestic flow of the universe.

***

Freeing Ourselves from the Shackles of the Past:

Living in the present moment is a profound practice that necessitates the liberation of our consciousness from the shackles of the past. Our minds often cling to memories, regrets, or experiences, creating a mental landscape that can hinder our ability to fully immerse ourselves in the current moment. To truly live in the present, it becomes imperative to cultivate a mindset that frees us from the burdens of what has come before.

One transformative approach is the practice of mindfulness. By becoming aware of our thoughts and gently redirecting our focus to the present, we create a space that allows us to break free from the entanglements of the past. Mindfulness encourages observing thoughts without judgment, acknowledging them, and then consciously choosing to shift our attention to the current moment. This practice empowers us to disentangle ourselves from the narrative of the past, fostering a sense of clarity and presence in the now.

Another powerful tool is the art of forgiveness. Often, we carry the weight of past grievances, whether towards ourselves or others. Forgiveness is not about condoning actions but about releasing the emotional hold these experiences have on our present. By letting go of resentment and embracing forgiveness, we create room for healing and open the door to a more liberated and present state of being.

Journaling is a liberating practice that can aid in the process of freeing ourselves from the past. Putting pen to paper allows us to externalize our thoughts and emotions, providing a tangible outlet for self-reflection. Through journaling, we can consciously address and release remaining thoughts about the past, allowing us to approach the present with a clearer and unburdened mind.

Mindful breathing exercises, such as meditation and deep breathing, serve as powerful tools to anchor ourselves in the present. Focusing on the breath enables us to center our awareness on the immediate sensations of the body, creating a mental sanctuary where the past loses its grip. Regular practice cultivates a heightened state of mindfulness, empowering us to navigate life with a renewed sense of clarity and presence.

Ultimately, the key lies in understanding that the past, while shaping our journey, does not define our present. It is a reservoir of lessons, not a prison. By embracing mindfulness, forgiveness, journaling, and conscious breathing, we untie ourselves from the web of the past, allowing the present moment to unfold with the richness and vitality it deserves. In this liberated state, we open ourselves to the fullness of the present, ready to engage with life's unfolding wonders.

Before we go any further, let me share with you very quick my personal journey of liberating myself from the burdens of the past, a practice that has been a profound and transformative experience. Though I humbly admit that claiming complete mastery over this process is beyond me, the steps I've taken suggest significant progress in my personality and in my relationships.

It was a few years ago when memories of a rocky relationship with a coworker ignited a flame of anger within me, creating a significant barrier to effective collaboration. It became evident that clutching onto these wrongs was a prevention to fostering a positive work environment and professional relationship.

Each meeting with this person became overwhelming for me. The memories of past pain caused by his wrongdoings dominated my thoughts and emotions. Instead of actively engaging in discussions and focusing on the tasks at hand, my mind nonstop replayed the harmful events and words.

This preoccupation not only obstructed my ability to contribute effectively but also posed a risk to the quality of my work, putting my job and career at considerable jeopardy. Living in past grievances became a significant obstacle, delaying both professional growth and the fulfillment of my responsibilities.

With a deliberate intention to overcome bitterness, I consciously chose to release the grip on resentment and offer forgiveness. Shifting my focus to the present, I approached each new interaction with this person as a new beginning, as if meeting him for the first time. This decision acted as a catalyst for a fresh start, leading to a remarkable transformation in the dynamics of our interaction. Simple greetings evolved into engaging small talk about current topics, ultimately fostering more effective collaboration on current work-related tasks. Surprisingly, these positive changes extended beyond the professional realm.

As our work relationship flourished, it organically spilled over into our personal lives. Beyond the confines of the workplace, we discovered shared interests and values, leading to the development of a genuine friendship.

Moreover, realizing that both of us hid similar feelings of resentment in the past further highlighted to me the significance of the positive changes initiated on my end.

In essence, this experience illuminated the transformative power of forgiveness and letting go, demonstrating that the decision to release the grip on past complaints not only mends professional relationships but can also foster genuine connections and friendship beyond the confines of the workplace.

Since this experience, I've made a conscious effort to embrace fresh starts in all aspects of my life, letting go of the past. It's an ongoing process, and while I haven't mastered it, I am committed to getting there eventually. Recognizing the significance of freeing myself from the shackles of the past and living in the moment, I've come to understand the importance of the art of living in the present as a powerful tool in harnessing the flow of the universe. When developing my own mantra, I ensured to incorporate this idea. Now, whenever I recite the mantra, I make a point to do it while fully immersed in the present, understanding that the act itself is a key element in aligning with the cosmic energies.

***

Freeing Ourselves from the Anxiety of the Future:

On the flip side, a nonstop preoccupation with the future can lead to anxiety and restlessness. The uncertainty of what lies ahead, coupled with the pressure to meet future expectations, or navigate potential challenges, can cast a looming shadow on our present experiences. Constantly worrying about what might happen can reduce from the joy and richness available in the here and now.

Indeed, the continuous chase of future milestones, while crucial for long-term success, often leads us to unintentionally neglect the richness of the present. It's a common narrative

– we set our sights on the next goal, eagerly anticipating the relief, joy, or satisfaction we believe will accompany its achievement. In doing so, we may unknowingly wish away the moments that make up our daily lives, allowing them to slip through our fingers unnoticed.

The habit of living for the future manifests in statements like, "I just can't wait for this to be over," or "I'll be happier once I get this done." These sentiments resonate with many of us, a testament to the predominant mindset that our current circumstances are purely difficulties to overcome on the path to a better, brighter future.

Whether it's pushing through a challenging day, eagerly awaiting the end of a month, or looking forward to vaction fun, the tendency is to view the present as a mere means to an end. The danger lies not only in the potential dissatisfaction upon reaching a goal but also in the continuous postponement of satisfaction. As one milestone is conquered, another swiftly takes its place, leaving us in a ceaseless cycle of striving.

The cost of this future-centric approach is high, and the bill comes due in the form of missed opportunities for joy, connection, and appreciation in the current moment. In our rush to fast-forward through the less glamorous aspects of life, we may unconsciously strip ourselves of the richness in the journey itself.

Moreover, the constant shifting of the goalpost reinforces the illusion that happiness is a destination, reachable only after overcoming the next challenge. The reality is that contentment, fulfillment, and joy can be found in the present, woven into the fabric of our everyday experiences.

The cure lies in cultivating mindfulness, an intentional awareness that allows us to fully engage with the present moment. It's about recognizing the beauty in the in-between moments, acknowledging the progress made, and finding gratitude for the journey, not just the destination.

By shifting our focus from "just getting through" to "fully experiencing," we reclaim the present as a source of fulfillment. It's a conscious choice to break free from the cycle of continuous striving, appreciating the here and now for what it is – a collection of moments that collectively shape our lives. In doing so, we learn to savor each step of the journey, finding contentment not just at the finish line but throughout the entire race.

Before we delve further, let me elaborate on my personal journey of liberating myself from the clutches of future anxiety—an endeavor that has proven profoundly transformative. While I humbly acknowledge that claiming complete mastery over this process remains elusive, the strides I've made signify substantial progress in the journey of life.

A couple of years ago, I faced a pivotal moment in my career—a highly important presentation that would significantly influence my future in the company. The looming pressure triggered my habitual worry about work presentations, amplifying my stress and preoccupying my thoughts with potential mishaps, judgment from others, and unfavorable outcomes.

During the intense stress, I went to a crucial family event, but I can't remember enjoying any moments. Even simple activities like eating and being with the people I love were overshadowed, as my mind was focused on the upcoming presentation.

Recognizing the harmful impact of this future anxiety, I embarked on a journey to liberate myself from its clutches. Instead of submitting to worries about the unknown future, I committed to a new approach. Focusing on the present moment and the immediate tasks at hand became my guiding principle. I meticulously broke down the preparation for the presentation into manageable steps, setting specific goals for each day leading up to the event. Importantly, I intentionally infused enjoyment into every single task, transforming the process from a daunting obligation to a fulfilling experience. Mindfulness techniques, including deep breathing and staying present, became my daily rituals to prevent my mind from wandering into anxious thoughts.

As the presentation day approached, I realized a profound shift in my mindset. Embracing each task with a newfound sense of enjoyment had a transformative effect. On the day of the presentation, I approached it with a remarkably calmer mindset—a mindset that surprisingly made the entire experience enjoyable. By redirecting my focus from the uncertainties of the future to the tasks at hand, I delivered the presentation with newfound confidence and effectiveness. The outcome surpassed my expectations.

This personal journey illuminated the power of liberating oneself from the clutches of future anxiety. The deliberate shift in perspective not only enhanced my performance but also allowed me to derive fulfillment from the present moment. It served as a reminder that embracing the present with intentionality and joy is not only a strategy for improved outcomes but a pathway to a more satisfying and enriching professional and personal life.

***

Freeing Ourselves from the Social and Cultural Pressure:

The currents of societal and cultural pressures also often conspire to divert our attention from the richness of the present moment as well. In a world fixated on success, achievements, and societal expectations, there exists a dominant mindset that the present is but a steppingstone, a means to an end in the ceaseless pursuit of milestones. The external pressures applied by the societal narrative push us into a perpetual state of striving, where each moment is perceived as an originator to the next achievement.

The persistent emphasis on measurable success and societal expectations acts as a powerful force, shaping our perspectives and influencing our priorities. The current of this collective mindset encourages a tunnel vision that consumes the future, overshadowing the value of the present journey. The result is a society caught in a constant cycle of goal setting, achievement-chasing, and a continuous craving for the next big accomplishment.

This constant striving not only amplifies stress and anxiety but also leaves limited room for the appreciation of the current journey. The very fabric of societal expectations weaves a narrative that measures worth in terms of future accomplishments, unintentionally dismissing the beauty and significance of the steps taken along the way.

To break free from this cultural stream, it requires a conscious reevaluation of priorities and a recalibration of perspective. It beckons individuals to challenge the prevailing narrative that success is solely defined by future achievements. Instead, there is a call to appreciate the present journey, recognizing that each step is a valuable destination in itself. By disentangling from the societal pressures that propel us forward relentlessly, we open the door to a more mindful and fulfilling existence—one where the present is not merely a means to an end but a destination worthy of profound appreciation.

My personal journey of freeing myself from social and cultural pressures finds its roots in a crucial decision my wife and I made early in our relationship. Recognizing the mutual passion, we shared for exploring the world, we deliberately chose to defy societal norms that often prescribe the accumulation of possessions like large houses and brand-new cars as the standard markers of success. Instead, we made a conscious decision to prioritize travel, acknowledging that experiences and memories hold far greater value for us than material possessions ever could.

This bold choice demanded that we release ourselves from the expectations imposed by society, expectations that place excessive emphasis on traditional measures of success. By challenging these norms head-on, we not only liberated ourselves from the pressure to conform to societal standards but also embraced a lifestyle in perfect alignment with our true interests and values.

This decision not only empowered us to actively pursue our shared love for travel but also underscored the vital importance of living in the present moment, choosing to savor experiences over deferring our dreams to an uncertain future. It has proven to be a continually liberating experience that shapes the course of our lives, serving as a perpetual reminder to prioritize meaningful experiences over societal expectations.

As we embraced our decision to prioritize travel and experiences over accumulating material possessions, an interesting dynamic unfolded. Those who had focused on buildup tangible items such as houses and cars began to look upon us with a tinge of envy. While we were savoring the richness of our present lives through exploration and meaningful experiences, they, despite their material wealth, found themselves longing for the joy and fulfillment that seemed to radiate from our chosen lifestyle.

This unforeseen reaction highlighted the contrast between societal expectations of success and the genuine contentment that can stem from aligning one's life with personal passions in the present time. Our choice not only liberated us from societal pressures but also unintentionally became a source of inspiration for others to live in the present.

In this way, our journey of freeing ourselves from societal expectations not only reshaped our own lives but also sparked reflections and reconsiderations in the lives of those around us.

This transformative journey further instilled in me the significance of living in the present, encouraging me to integrate this awareness into my personal mantra. As I recite my mantra and reach the part where I list my wishes, I intentionally begin by envisioning the next destinations my wife and I yearn to explore. By doing so, I actively connect with the universe, inviting it to manifest these enriching experiences in my current present. This deliberate choice rejects the notion of postponing joy to an uncertain future, acknowledging that the optimal time to relish life is now. It's a practice that reinforces the idea that living in the present is not just a philosophical concept but a tangible and influential force in shaping the quality of our experiences and the fulfillment we derive from them.

***

In the conclusion of this exploration into the art of living in the present as a powerful tool for harnessing the flow of the universe, we arrive at a fundamental truth – the practice of reciting our mantra becomes an exquisite dance with the cosmos when infused with the essence of the present moment. Once we have crafted and developed our mantra, it is not merely a sequence of words but a vibrant outlet that connects us to the rhythmic pulse of the universe.

The universe, in all its majesty, invites us to engage with the present, shedding the weight of the past and the uncertainty of the future. To truly harness the flow of the universe, we must cast off the shackles of past regrets and release the grip of future anxieties.

Living in the present is the key – a conscious choice to savor each breath, to embrace the in-between moments, and to revel in the beauty of the now. As we utter our mantra, it becomes more than a series of sounds; it transforms into a vibrant expression of our existence, resonating with the universal energies that surround us. The mantra, when recited in the present, establishes a profound connection, like a harmonious chord in the grand symphony of existence.

To fully harness the flow of the universe, we must liberate ourselves from the societal controls that often dictate the trajectory of our lives. The pressures to obey to external standards can obscure the clarity of the present moment. Breaking free from these societal currents allows us to navigate our own course, aligning our journey with the cosmic rhythms rather than the expectations of others.

In conclusion, the art of living in the present emerges not only as a harmonizing practice but as a crucial aspect of our transformative journey. As we recite our mantra with mindfulness, free from the burdens of the past and unencumbered by the anxieties of the future, we create a profound connection with the universe. It is in the present moment that the universe opens its arms to us, inviting us to participate in the ever-flowing dance of existence. In this dance, we find not only a deeper connection with the cosmos but the extraordinary ability to harness the majestic flow of the universe itself.

2 FEELING GOOD

Advancing in our mission to study the cosmic symphony of the universe, we gracefully transition into the second chapter of our exploration. Here, we continue to dig deeper into my mantra, unveiling additional tools that assist us in understanding our fundamental role in shaping our own reality. Resuming from where we left off in the previous chapter with the mantra, "and I'm now so HAPPY and feel so GOOD," we recognize it as yet another invitation to explore the profound significance of vocalizing our emotional state. This revelation positions uttering our feelings as an essential tool in mastering the dance of universal alignment.

Similar to a symphony's unfolding tale through a continuous melody, the journey of harnessing the universe's flow develops with each note of the mantra. These apparently simple words grow into a vibrant buildup, resonating with the fabric of our existence. The mantra is more than affirmations; it acts as a guide through complex emotional passages, urging us to become skillful conductors in life's grand orchestra.

The exploration in this chapter exceeds the surface of mere recitation, urging us to understand the mantra as a living, breathing expression of our inner state. As we delve into the essence of feeling HAPPY and GOOD, we discover the realization that our emotional landscape is not a passive setting but an active force capable of influencing the cosmic vibrations that shape our reality. These words become the brushstrokes on the canvas of our existence, painting a picture of alignment with the harmonious energies that fill out the universe.

Building upon the previous chapter, we address the notion that our emotional state is not just a significance of external circumstances; it is a dynamic force that actively contributes to the co-creation of our experiences. By expressing our happiness and well-being, we engage in a conscious dialogue with the universe, declaring our readiness to participate in the cosmic ballet of manifestation.

In the symphony of universal alignment, the mantra goes beyond being a tool—it becomes a deep acknowledgment of our ability to shape the rhythms of our destiny. It encourages us to realize that, like skilled musicians, we can adjust our emotional frequencies to align with the cosmic pace. As we explore further, we see the mantra not just as words but as a crucial part of the larger score, urging us to harmonize with the cosmic melodies that resonate throughout existence.

***

The Power of Emotional Declaration:

In understanding the power embedded within the act of emotional declaration, we unveil a truth that exceeds the superficiality of words.

"and I'm so HAPPY and feel so GOOD" becomes more than a mere sequence; it transforms into a deliberate proclamation, a resonant declaration that echoes through the cosmos, revealing the depth of our prevailing emotions. It is, in essence, a cosmic conversation initiated by our emotional state.

By verbalizing feelings of happiness and well-being, we engage in an intentional act of setting a vibrational frequency that resonates with the vast cosmic orchestra. This proclamation is a signal to the universe, a communication that extends beyond the boundaries of spoken language. It is a declaration of our readiness to align with positive energies, creating a harmonious collaboration between our internal vibrations and the universal currents conducive to manifestation.

In essence, the power of emotional declaration is a recognition of our intervention in the grand design of the universe. It is an acknowledgment that our emotions are not passive reactions but dynamic forces that shape the very reality we experience. As we express happiness and well-being through the mantra, we become active participants in the cosmic dialogue, co-authoring the narrative of our existence in collaboration with the vast, harmonious energies of the universe.

***

Crafting Alignment Even in Harshness:

In our emotional symphony, the mantra teaches a significant lesson. It goes beyond the joyful harmonies and digs into the conflicting realms. It teaches us that, even when our emotions clash with happiness, we have the power to create alignment amidst the harshness. This realization is a crucial understanding, revealing our profound capacity to make intentional choices even when faced with dissonance.

The mantra becomes a helpful structure that emphasizes the significance of "Fake it until you make it." This phrase takes on a profound meaning, transforming into more than a casual suggestion and evolving into a transformative mantra itself. It means not a deception of our true emotions but a conscious choice to excel the dissonance, initiating a deliberate act of alignment with the cosmic rhythms that govern the universe.

Choosing joy, even amidst challenging moments, becomes an intentional act of co-creation with the universe. It is a courageous step that exceeds the reactive nature of emotions, pushing us into the realm of deliberate creators of our destiny. The transformative process is set into motion as we consciously select the emotional frequencies we wish to originate, signaling to the cosmos our commitment to aligning with positive energies even when faced with misfortune.

As we courageously navigate harsh moments with the intention to align with joy, we step into the role of co-creators with the universe. We become active participants in the dance of creation, harnessing the power within ourselves to shape the harmonious melodies of our destiny, even when faced with the discordant notes of life's challenges.

***

Feeling Good Beyond the Mantra:

Creating a positive emotional state goes beyond mantra recitation; it becomes a daily practice, a commitment to infuse every moment with the uplifting energy of joy. This isn't just about repeating a mantra; it's a living, breathing experience that profoundly influences our entire being.

To enhance our mantra's impact on harnessing the universe's flow, we begin a journey where feeling good is a crucial aspect of our daily story. This isn't about ignoring our true emotions but about consciously selecting and nurturing a positive emotional state. It recognizes that our emotions actively shape the vibrations we send out into the cosmic dance.

Bringing joy into every part of our lives is a collaborative effort with the universe. It means intentionally selecting thoughts, actions, and perspectives that align with harmonious energies, fostering manifestation. This ongoing practice extends across different aspects of our lives, from the everyday to the extraordinary.

In my personal journey of exploring the profound impact of feeling happy on harnessing the flow of the universe, one significant aspect stands out—financial abundance. A few years ago, my financial landscape was marked by challenges, with debts looming and a prevailing sense of scarcity casting a shadow over my life. Acknowledging the need for a profound change, I made a conscious decision to integrate feelings of financial security and gratitude into my daily existence.

Understanding the transformative power of feeling good, especially in the context of financial well-being, became a focal point of my journey. I not only embraced this mindset within the limits of my mantra but also actively practiced it throughout my daily activities. Whether through moments of reflection, expressions of gratitude, or intentional focus on positive aspects of my financial situation, I engrossed myself in the energy of abundance.

This deliberate integration of feeling good into my routine wasn't just a phony addition; it was a conscious effort to align my internal state with the flow of the universe. As I consistently practiced gratitude and nurtured a positive mindset, the transformative effects became evident. The once burdensome financial challenges began to shift, making way for unexpected opportunities, successful financial decisions, and an overall improvement in my financial circumstances. Suddenly, opportunities seemed to materialize out of nowhere. Savings presented themselves everywhere I turned. Wise financial decisions became a consistent theme, and an influx of free resources became a regular occurrence.

This experience has taught me that feeling happy and grateful is not merely a reaction to external circumstances; it is a proactive force that can shape and attract the very circumstances we desire. Financial abundance is not just about the numbers on a balance sheet; it's a reflection of the alignment between our internal state of being and the cosmic flow of prosperity.

***

Daily Practices for Infusing Joy:

In the next part of this chapter, I will outline several strategies that have played a crucial role in shifting my feelings, particularly in the previous personal example. My sincere hope is that these strategies will offer guidance and support, empowering you to navigate through difficulties by transforming your emotional landscape.

1. Gratitude Rituals: Concluding each day with a practice of expressing gratitude for the positive aspects of life. This intentional act shifts focus from worry to appreciation, setting a positive tone for both the day and overall life.

2. Mindfulness Exercises: Engaging in meditation and other mindfulness activities to anchor ourselves in the present moment, fostering an awareness that allows joy to naturally permeate our consciousness.

3. Positive Affirmations: Integrating uplifting affirmations into our daily

routine to consciously direct our thoughts towards positivity and well-being.

4. Connect with Nature: Spending time outdoors, appreciating the beauty of nature. Nature has a profound ability to evoke a sense of joy and tranquility.

5. Acts of Kindness: Performing small acts of kindness for others, as the act of giving and spreading joy contributes to our own sense of fulfillment.

6. Physical Exercise: Regular physical activity releases endorphins, fostering a sense of well-being and happiness.

7. Connect with Loved Ones: Meaningful connections and shared moments with friends and family contribute significantly to emotional well-being.

By weaving these practices into the fabric of our daily lives, feeling good becomes more than a fleeting emotion—it transforms into a state of being.

The mantra, when recited in harmony with this continuous practice, becomes a powerful tool in amplifying the joyous frequencies we release into the universe. In doing so, we become architects of our own emotional resonance, forging a harmonious connection with the cosmic energies that surround us. This dynamic relationship establishes the base for a life where the art of feeling good is not just a sporadic occurrence but a continuous symphony that orchestrates our journey towards harnessing the flow of the universe.

As we conclude this chapter, the significance of the mantra echoes louder – feeling good is not just a brief emotion; it is a deliberate choice, a continuous practice, and a powerful tool for aligning with the universe's flow. By declaring our happiness and well-being, we step into the role of architects, shaping our reality in harmony with the cosmic design.

3 GRATITUDE

In the third chapter of our exploration, we discover another important tool in the mantra—expressing gratitude and its reciprocal dance - "the more you give, the more you get."

We continue breaking down the mantra introduced in the introduction, focusing on the part that says, "and I'm so HAPPY and feel so GOOD, because of how far I've come in my life and because of all the great things coming my way right now. I'm blessed, appreciative, grateful, and thankful for everything I have, all I had, all the experiences I went through, and everything I'm going through right now."

As we continue to explore the parts of the mantra, let's break down this part of the mantra to understand the role of gratitude in harnessing the flow of the universe:

***

"I'm so HAPPY and feel so GOOD": This section of the mantra, as discussed before, is like a sunrise, bringing warmth and joy to our thoughts and feelings. It's like opening a door to a room filled with sunshine, instantly brightening our inner world with positivity. This declaration is a tuning of our inner frequencies to resonate with happiness and well-being, creating a harmonious symphony within.

***

"Because of how far I've come in my life": This thoughtful phrase invites us to look back at our life's journey, acknowledging the significant odyssey we've experienced. It's a reflection filled with self-awareness, recognizing the profound changes within us. As we engage in self-reflection, we warmly appreciate the expansive path we've traveled.

The essence of this passage is acknowledging personal growth, likened to perusing the pages of a captivating autobiography. Each step, stumble, and triumph adds to the evolving narrative. It's a celebration not only of the journey's physical distance but also of the deepening understanding, resilience, and wisdom gained along the way.

Gratitude becomes a supportive companion here, a guiding star illuminating both milestones and challenges. It's more than a passing emotion; it's a genuine acknowledgment of our transformative journey. This phrase resonates with appreciating life's lessons, where growth isn't a mere concept but a living evidence to our resilience and ability to transform.

Personally, as I recite the part of the mantra acknowledging my humble family, town, and upbringing, I take pride in reflecting on my life's accomplishments and appreciate the progress I've made in various aspects such as romance, education, career, finances and more.

***

"And because of all the great things coming my way right now": Shifting to the present, gratitude expands beyond past achievements. It becomes a vivid canvas, painted with the colors of the current moment and woven with threads of possibilities and blessings yet to unfold. In this moment, the heart swells with appreciation for both past milestones and the open chapters awaiting our touch.

Gratitude, like a bright sun, enhances the present's potential. It's a melody for both past and current achievements, a dance with opportunities, celebrating the joys of today.

In this passage, gratitude becomes a vital element in our ongoing narrative. It acknowledges not only what has transpired but also the dynamic and evolving present. The phrase encapsulates the spirit of being mindfully present, as gratitude navigates us through the unexplored territories of the present, allowing us to appreciate the beauty of the unfolding journey, moment by moment.

When I personally recite this part of the mantra, it feels like a fountain of possibilities, where my dreams and desires come to life. It's as if the universe is rearranging itself to present exactly what I want on a silver plate.

***

"I'm blessed, appreciative, grateful, and thankful": Each of these four descriptors unfolds a distinct side of the gratitude. "Blessed" casts a radiant light on the sense of divine favor that graces our existence, portraying life as a given gift, woven with threads of celestial kindness. It captures the acknowledgment that we are recipients of a divine dance, where each step is guided by unseen hands, composing our journey with celestial elegance.

"Appreciative," in its powerful simplicity, signifies a conscious recognition of the inherent value scattered across the landscape of our experiences. It's a nod to the treasures hidden in plain sight, a whisper of gratitude for the richness embedded in the seemingly ordinary moments of life. This term opens our eyes to the beauty that resides in the details, inviting us to cherish the beautiful shades of our existence.

Moving along the spectrum, "grateful" deepens the emotional resonance of thankfulness. It unveils a source of profound gratitude, an acknowledgment that stretches beyond the surface, touching the very core of our being. It's an emotive expression of thanks, a heartbeat echoing the profound connection we share with the sophistications of life.

Lastly, "thankful" acts as the key player, uniting acknowledgment and appreciation into a harmonious symphony. It represents the active engagement of recognizing the gifts that life gives upon us and responding with a heart full of gratitude.

These descriptors come together like a poetic song dedicated to gratitude, forming a language that beautifully expresses the multifaceted beauty found in acknowledging, appreciating, and giving thanks for the intricate dance of existence.

Growing up, I was brought up with the belief that expressing gratitude is not just a courtesy but a profound means of genuinely delivering appreciation. This early influence played a substantial role in shaping my approach when creating my mantra. With a conscious and deliberate choice, I chose to fill a diverse range of expressions such as being blessed, appreciative, grateful, and thankful into my mantra. The purpose behind this decision was to not only emphasize but also to showcase the profound depth of gratitude that resides within me. I hold the belief that this intentional emphasis on gratitude is active in enriching the overall effectiveness of the mantra, transforming it into a powerful and influential tool for harnessing the flow of the universe.

***

"For everything I have, all I had, all the experiences I went through, and everything I'm going through right now": This broad expression of gratitude unfolds like a heartfelt melody, resonating with appreciation for the present, the echoes of the past, and the rhythmic beats of the ongoing journey.

Gratitude for current possessions paints a canvas decorated with the colors of satisfaction and abundance. It is the recognition and celebration of the blessings that surround us in the immediate moment — a sincere acknowledgment of the richness embedded in our lives. This side of gratitude is like a warm embrace, acknowledging the tangible gifts we hold in our hands and the intangible joys that grace our daily existence.

In my daily recitation of the mantra, my mind naturally goes through the tangible possessions that I'm fortunate to own, including homeownership, reliable transportation, and essential technological tools like a laptop and

WIFI. Additionally, I express gratitude for the communication device, my cell phone, that keeps me connected with loved ones.

sometimes, I also take a moment to reflect on the symbolic possessions that many may not have, such as a shelter, access to clean water, clothing, food, and the warmth within my home. These reflections serve as a reminder of the basic necessities that not everyone enjoys.

These daily contemplations play a crucial role in nurturing a deeper appreciation for both the material and symbolic aspects of my life. They contribute to fostering a profound sense of contentment and abundance, enhancing the overall effectiveness of my mantra in harnessing the flow of the universe.

When extending gratitude to past experiences, both positive and challenging, the narrative becomes richer. It's a reflective journey through the records of personal history, appreciating the sunny peaks of joy and the shadowed valleys of challenges. Gratitude for positive experiences becomes a celebration of growth, lessons learned, and moments that have shaped the core of who we are. Simultaneously, gratitude for challenging experiences represents a courageous acknowledgment of the strength derived from hardship, revealing the transformative power embedded in life's trials.

When I reflect on this part of the mantra, my mind doesn't focus on the hardships I've encountered in life but rather on how these challenges have shaped the person I am today. For instance, the experience of coming to a new country and starting a new life was undoubtedly challenging, but it presented me with an opportunity to develop resilience and adaptability. It is through overcoming such hurdles that I've grown into a reliable individual, trusted with the responsibility of running a multi-million-dollar business. This perspective emphasizes the transformative power of challenges and contributes to a deeper sense of gratitude and acknowledgment during my mantra recitation.

Also, when contemplating this section of the mantra, I make sure to recall some of the remarkable experiences that have contributed to shaping the person I am today. One standout memory is the participation in an incredible fellowship program several years ago. Over the course of six months, I collaborated with over 40 participants from more than 30 countries worldwide, engaging in a rich exchange of experiences. This transformative experience significantly enriched my personality, fostering a deep understanding of diverse cultures. It turned me into a multi-cultural competent individual, sparking my eagerness to explore more cultures, travel the world, and confidently navigate multi-cultural situations. This reflection adds a layer of appreciation for the impactful experiences that have molded my character.

Back to the mantra, and as the gaze shifts towards the ongoing journey, the expression of gratitude unfolds like a map unrolling its vast territories. It summarizes the anticipation of the unknown, the thrill of possibilities, and the acknowledgment that the journey itself is a precious gift. Gratitude here is an active and dynamic force, shaping the trajectory of the path ahead with a heart open to the wonders yet to unfold.

In essence, this comprehensive gratitude becomes a symphony that harmonizes the past, present, and future notes of our lives. It is a melody that celebrates the richness of the entire journey — from the treasures held in the now to the pearls of wisdom strung along the thread of our experiences, creating a harmonious composition that resounds with gratitude.

***

As we draw the curtain on this chapter, it is imperative to offer valuable insights for those embarking on the creation of their own mantra to tap into the cosmic flow. An essential piece of advice is to lay the cornerstone of your mantra with gratitude, placing significant emphasis on the unwavering belief that the more you give, the more you receive.

This foundational gratitude is not limited but expansive, enveloping the sum of your existence across time—acknowledging the past, embracing the present, and anticipating the future. Let your expressions of gratitude extend to both material possessions and the series of experiences that weave the intricate tapestry of your journey. Cultivate thankfulness for all that has been a part of your life and for everything that currently graces your existence.

The true essence lies in aligning your mantra with the flow of the universe. This involves filling your words with a genuine and comprehensive gratitude that resonates with the energies of the cosmos. This deliberate alignment serves as a catalyst, increasing the effectiveness of your mantra. Your mantra, enriched by profound gratitude, transforms into a powerful tool capable of shaping your reality. It acts as a magnetic force, drawing positive energies and establishing a profound connection with the abundant flow of the universe. Through this intentional practice, your mantra becomes a dynamic tool, empowering you to actively co-create a reality filled with positivity, abundance, and a deep sense of appreciation.

4 AFFIRMATION

As we enter this chapter, let's pause momentarily from our exploration of the breaking down my own mantra into introducing a powerful tool that adds another dimension to our journey of harnessing the flow of the universe—the Rule of Affirmation.

Affirmations, the practice of positive self-statements and declarations, play a profound role in shaping our mindset, influencing our actions, and ultimately, empowering us to align with the cosmic currents.

In this chapter, we steer our focus toward the rule of affirmation and its transformative potential. Affirmations, whether rooted in mantras or integrated into various aspects of our lives, become the threads that weave the fabric of our reality. By understanding and harnessing the rule of affirmation, we unlock a tool that amplifies the effectiveness of our mantra.

Join me in this exploration as we untie the principles behind affirmations, their role in shaping our thoughts and actions, and how they serve as a dynamic force in our quest to align with the abundant flow of the universe. Together, let us discover the empowering capabilities that affirmations bring to our journey, guiding us toward the supreme goal of harnessing the boundless energies of the universe.

In the moments when we first open our eyes to greet a new day, we are presented with a choice—a choice that has the potential to shape the course of our hours and the trajectory of our lives. This choice is the decision to hold the transformative power of positive morning affirmations, a practice that not only sets the tone for our day but also attracts to us the powerful energies of love, joy, abundance, success, and harmony.

Positive affirmations, particularly those embraced in the morning, can be likened to keys unlocking a treasure chest abundant with the riches of the universe. These affirmations, although simple in structure, possess profound power. When spoken with purpose and belief, they inject our consciousness with a shining positivity that fills every aspect of our being. Through the practice of intentional affirmation, we tap into a fountain of positive energy that sets a harmonious tone for the day, fostering a mindset encouraging to attracting abundance, joy, and success.

As we stand before the mirror, brush our teeth, or sip our morning coffee, we have the opportunity to speak into existence the realities we wish to create. By listening to and reciting affirmations that resonate with our hearts, we invite the energy of love, joy, and abundance to flow into our lives like a gentle stream, nourishing our souls and enriching our experiences.

By listening to or uttering these positive morning affirmations with unwavering belief and repeating them daily, we align ourselves with the energies of love, joy, abundance, success, and harmony. These affirmations become the mantras that guide our day, the compass that directs our intentions, and the bridge that connects us to the limitless possibilities that await us.

So, let us rise each morning with a heart full of gratitude and a spirit brimming with positivity. As we listen to these affirmations and declare our intentions, we welcome the powerful energies of the universe into our lives, setting the stage for a day filled with love, joy, abundance, success, and harmony.

***

Example of Morning Affirmation:

97

In the upcoming section of this chapter, we will delve into a practical example of a positive affirmation that holds the potential to be a guiding light in our daily lives. This affirmation can be listened to or recited each morning, serving as a powerful tool to harness the flow of the universe and set a harmonious tone for the day ahead.

As we explore this affirmation, we will uncover its significance, dissect its components, and understand how it can become a source of inspiration, strength, and alignment with the greater rhythms of existence. By incorporating such affirmations into our daily routines, we can tap into the ever-flowing stream of the universe, harmonizing our intentions with its grand design.

Here's the example: " As I start my day, I embrace it with love and gratitude. Thankful for the gift of life, my heart is open to all the positivity around me. I radiate love, joy, and kindness, serving as a beacon of inspiration. Today, I welcome the abundance that comes my way, and my day is filled with appreciation. Choosing happiness, I affirm that I am a loving, positive, and amazing person. A good soul, an awesome being, and a powerful creator, I shape the life I desire. Miracles manifest for me, making today special—a gift to be celebrated with gratitude. I love myself and others unconditionally, spreading kindness and believing in my potential. Successful, intuitive, and wise, I validate myself and fulfill my purpose. Joyful, abundant, and peaceful, I align with universal energy, allowing harmony to flow within me. Today is limitless, filled with positive happenings, expected and unexpected. Life is a wonder, and I am truly blessed. Thank you, thank you for this precious day and my beautiful life."

Now, let us take a closer look and break down this positive affirmation to gain a deeper understanding of how it functions and why it becomes effective in our mission to harness the flow of the universe. To fully grasp its transformative power, we'll divide its components, examining each element's role in shaping our mindset and aligning us with the cosmic rhythms.

By breaking down the affirmation in this way, we gain a comprehensive understanding of how it operates as a tool for harnessing the flow of the universe. It is not merely a collection of words; it is a dynamic instrument for reshaping our consciousness and aligning our intentions with the grand symphony of existence. In the following sections, we will explore the practical steps for integrating this affirmation into our daily lives, allowing its transformative power to guide us on our journey.

In the previous example of a positive affirmation, as we begin our day, we are filled with a profound sense of love and gratitude. It is a gentle reminder that being alive is a precious gift, a chance to engage ourselves with the existence. With an open heart, we embrace the day that stretches before us, a canvas of endless possibilities.

In this moment, we are shining beacons of love, joy, and kindness. Our intention is clear: to radiate these qualities into the world and touch the lives of those we encounter. With each breath, we are mindful of the love that flows within us, the joy that bubbles in our hearts, and the kindness that extends from our souls.

Today, we allow all the good that the universe has in store for us to flow effortlessly into our lives. Our hearts are magnets, attracting appreciation and positivity like a beacon in the night. We choose happiness as our companion, and we carry it with us throughout the day, sharing it with everyone we meet.

In this moment, we are amazing people with good and compassionate souls. We are filled with a deep sense of awe for the beauty of life and the boundless potential within us. We are awesome and powerful creators, crafting the life we truly want to live with each thought, each action, and each intention.

Today, we anticipate miracles manifesting before our very eyes. It is a special day, a gift to be celebrated. We are overflowing with love for ourselves and others, embracing the world with kindness, believing in the inherent goodness of humanity.

Today, we validate ourselves, recognizing our worthiness and unique gifts. We are fulfilling our potentials, guided by intuition and wisdom. We are giving ourselves the love, care, and attention we deserve.

Joy fills every corner of our being as we move through this day. Abundance surrounds us, and peace envelops our souls. We are aligned and connected to the universal energy that flows within us, and we allow it to guide us on this remarkable journey.

Today, we are in harmony with the universe, acknowledging that we are limitless in our capacity to love, create, and thrive. The day unfolds with a symphony of positivity, with both expected and unexpected blessings gracing our path.

We celebrate the wonderment and appreciation that fill every moment. We are profoundly blessed, and we express our gratitude for this day and for our precious life. With a heart full of thanks, we step into the world, ready to embrace all that this day has to offer. Thank you, thank you for this day, for our life, and for all the blessings that are yet to come.

In essence, this positive affirmation is a holistic practice that combines gratitude, positivity, and self-affirmation to create a mindset conducive to attracting positivity and abundance throughout the day.

***

As we're concluding this chapter, I would like to share with you my own experience with affirmations. In my journey to harness the flow of the universe, I discovered very early on just how powerful and effective affirmations can be. They have a unique ability to make us feel good, happy, and open to the universe's transformative influence.

Affirmations, as simple as they may seem, possess an extraordinary power to reshape our thinking, emotions, and ultimately, our reality. They serve as the bridge between our inner desires and the boundless possibilities of the universe. My own journey with affirmations has been a evidence to the remarkable impact these positive statements can have on our lives.

I began my quest by searching the internet and diving into the massive sea of affirmations available online. It was essential for me to find the affirmations that resonated deeply with my heart, soothing my worries and doubts, while also confirming the profound truth that I am the creator of my destiny and future. The beauty of affirmations lies in their diversity – there are affirmations tailored to almost every aspect of life, from financial abundance to personal growth and emotional healing. I was able to select those that spoke to my unique aspirations and challenges, creating a personalized roadmap for my inner transformation.

What I quickly discovered was that the mere act of repeating these affirmations had a profound effect on my daily life. They became a powerful tool to shift my mindset. The positive messages began to dissolve the cloud of negativity and self-doubt that had lingered for far too long. Instead, they paved the way for feelings of self-worth, confidence, and empowerment.

Affirmations also served as a daily reminder of my role as a co-creator with the universe. I realized that I held the power to steer the ship of my life in any direction I chose. This newfound sense of agency was exhilarating, and it filled me with a deep sense of purpose and optimism.

One of the most remarkable transformations I experienced was the impact on my overall happiness and well-being. Affirmations possess a unique power to generate positive feelings and happiness. By consistently focusing on the positive aspects of life, my perspective shifted from one of scarcity to one of abundance. I began to notice the beauty in everyday moments, appreciating the small joys that had previously gone unnoticed.

These affirmations were more than just words; they acted as a beacon guiding me toward a more joyful and fulfilled life. They allowed me to open my heart and mind to the universe's transformative influence. I soon realized that the universe responds to the energy I release, and as I radiated positivity and belief, it seemed to conspire in my favor.

My financial circumstances began to improve as my affirmations nurtured a mindset of abundance. Opportunities I had never imagined started to present themselves. What had once been financial worries gradually transformed into a landscape marked by wealth and prosperity.

In addition to the tangible changes in my life, my relationships experienced a profound change. The positivity and self-assuredness I gained through affirmations rippled outwards, creating more harmonious and fulfilling connections with others. I became a magnet for like-minded individuals who shared my newfound sense of optimism.

In conclusion, my journey with affirmations has been a remarkable one. These positive statements have been a guiding light on my path of self-discovery and transformation. They have the power to shape our consciousness, influence our emotions, and bring about tangible changes in our lives. Affirmations are not mere words but keys that unlock the doors to our own potential and the universe's limitless possibilities.

As we conclude this chapter, I encourage you to explore the transformative power of affirmations in your own life. Find the affirmations that resonate with your heart, and with consistency, sincerity, and belief, incorporate them into your daily routine. You'll soon discover that, like me, you hold the ability to feel good, happy, and open to the universe's transformative influence, as you embark on a journey of inner and outer transformation. The universe eagerly awaits your intentions, ready to co-create a reality that resonates with the deepest desires of your heart and the infinite flow of the cosmos.

5 BELIEVING IN THE BELIEF

In this chapter, we will delve into the transformative power of belief and its profound influence on our ability to harness the flow of the universe. The focus will be on the concept of "believing in the belief," exploring how our beliefs shape our reality.

This discussion is involvedly connected to our ongoing breakdown of the mantra, providing a holistic understanding of the elements that contribute to aligning with the universe's energies. As we analyze the layers of belief, we uncover a fundamental aspect that plays a crucial role in our journey towards the supreme goal outlined in this book.

At the heart of this exploration lies a specific passage from the mantra: "And I know, like I know, like I know with unwavering faith..." This statement serves as a gateway to understanding the unwavering faith that acts as a catalyst in shaping our reality. We will unravel the layers of certainty embedded in this declaration and explore how it drives us towards a harmonious connection with the cosmic flow.

***

The Belief as a Transformative Force:

By examining the core of belief, we would recognize it not merely as an intellectual process but as a powerful force that holds the potential to bring about profound transformations. We explore the dynamics of belief and how it extends beyond a mental concept to become a driving factor in shaping our experiences and interactions with the universe.

Building upon the foundational understanding of belief, we examine its role in shaping our perception of reality. By acknowledging the complicated connection between belief and perception, we unlock the door to a deeper understanding of how our beliefs act as filters, influencing the energies we attract from the universe. This exploration illuminates the symbiotic relationship between our beliefs and the unfolding cosmic narrative.

Drawing the threads together, we establish a clear link between our beliefs and the universe's response. By comprehending this connection, we gain valuable insights into how belief acts as a powerful tool in harnessing the flow of the universe.

***

I Know, like I Know, Like I Know:

To better understand, let's analyze a specific passage from the mantra. We will focus on the repetition of the phrase "like I know" to emphasize a strong certainty. We will delve into the shades of this declaration, uncovering the levels of belief and confidence it conveys. Through a close examination of the language, we can gain insights into the profound belief expressed in this part of the mantra.

Going deeper, we delve into the layers of certainty and faith embedded in the mantra. We examine how the repetition acts as more than just words, but as a strong reinforcement of unshakable belief. This exploration sheds light on the significant influence of absolute certainty and faith in aligning with the universe's energy.

Building on the examined passage, we extend the discussion to encompass the wider concept of events happening for a reason. By recognizing the characteristic purpose and positivity behind life's events, we align ourselves with the flow of the universe. We delve into the transformative power of interpreting events through the lens of faith and reason, highlighting how this mindset contributes to the overarching goal of harnessing the cosmic flow.

***

The Great Reason:

Back to the part of the mantra that discuss: "all this is happening for a reason, a good reason, actually it's a great reason," we come across a profound idea of the "great reason" which governs the events of life. It is a notion that every experience, whether positive or challenging, carries a purposeful underpinning.

By understanding and embracing the concept of a "great reason," we can navigate through the difficulties of life with a heightened sense of purpose and optimism. This exploration sheds light on the transformative potential inherent in perceiving life events through the lens of a greater purpose.

Building on the "great reason" concept, we acknowledge the positive reason behind life events contributes to the harmonious flow of the universe. By recognizing the inherent goodness and purpose in every circumstance, we align ourselves with the positive energies of the cosmos. This mindset shift fosters a sense of co-creation with the universe, inviting a flood of abundance and positivity into our lives.

By this point, we realize that we need a transformative mindset shift in which challenges are viewed as opportunities for growth and learning. By reframing hardship as a steppingstone toward the fulfillment of a "great reason," we can navigate challenges with resilience and optimism. This shift in perspective not only enhances our ability to harness the flow of the universe but also empowers us to extract valuable lessons from every experience, further enriching their life journey.

On my quest to comprehend the profound reasons behind life's challenges and hardships, I, like many, encounter moments of frustration in the face of hardship. Yet, I try my best to foster the habit of perceiving these challenges not only as momentary setbacks but as opportunities for a greater good.

Rather than waiting for hindsight to reveal the purpose behind difficulties, I try to shift my perspective in the present moment. I'm working on myself to view hardships as unfolding narratives with reasons that will become clear in due time. To reinforce this mindset, I often recall past experiences where initially challenging circumstances ultimately led to positive outcomes.

For instance, the decision to leave my home country and relocate to the United States initially posed numerous challenges. However, looking back, I realize that this move paved the way for me to meet my life partner, my wife, and initiate a transformative chapter in my life. Similarly, enduring years of living alone taught me resilience and reliability, qualities that have shaped the person I am today.

Another instance involves a significant career change a couple of years ago, a move that initially seemed unproductive. However, with time, I came to understand that this period of professional transition equipped me with priceless skills and knowledge, particularly in accounting and sales aspects, that I wouldn't have acquired otherwise. This shift became a steppingstone to my current role, where I am more proficient and resourceful, showcasing how what seemed like a setback at the time was, in fact, a crucial building block for personal and professional growth.

This perspective on challenges as opportunities for a great reason has become a guiding principle in my intentional living journey, reinforcing my belief in the unfolding cosmic dance and the underlying harmony that connects all aspects of life.

***

Unwavering Faith and Manifestation:

The more we dig into harnessing the flow of the universe, the more we come to a clear realization that the unwavering faith has a transformative influence to spark manifestation. Unwavering faith goes beyond mere belief to become an active force in bringing desires and intentions into reality. By understanding the strength of committed faith, we unravel the dynamics through which unwavering faith becomes a driving factor in the manifestation process.

To provide tangible insights, this section incorporates an example from my own life that illustrate the profound impact of unwavering faith on manifestation.

In the first example, in 2022, I found myself at the lowest point in my career. Economic downturns and personal challenges led to the loss of everything my wife and I had built. My confidence was shattered, and conventional wisdom suggested that rebuilding from such a rock bottom would be an impossible task.

Instead of submitting to misery, I turned inward to my unwavering faith. Despite the chaos surrounding me, I held an unwavering belief that this setback was not the end but a necessary pause for a greater purpose. My faith became a beacon, guiding me through the darkest times and introducing hope where there seemed to be none.

With unwavering faith in my heart, I embarked on the challenging path of rebuilding. Beginning anew, I utilized my skills, past experiences, and the wisdom gained from adversity. I saw every obstacle as an opportunity for a comeback, and my steadfast belief provided the resilience required to maneuver through the process of rebuilding a career from the bottom up.

Slowly but steadily, my career began to regain momentum. Opportunities emerged that seemed almost miraculous, and my unwavering faith pushed me forward. I embraced challenges as steppingstones, and each small success became a testament to the transformative power of maintaining faith in the face of adversity.

Against all odds, my career not only recovered but soared to new heights. The unwavering faith that guided me through the toughest times manifested into remarkable achievements. I not only reached the pinnacle of my past success but surpassed it, doubling my highest level of achievement. My journey became a living testimony to the incredible resilience that unwavering faith can instill.

Now, at the peak of my career, I've become an inspiration to those facing similar challenges. Through sharing my story of resilience, I've ignited a spark in others to believe in their potential and navigate their own setbacks with unwavering faith. My journey serves as a beacon of hope, demonstrating that even from the depths of despair, one can rise, rebuild, and achieve unimaginable success.

My own example stands as a tiny one compared millions of stories that we hear about every day. We just need to listen and believe in them and try to copy them in our own lives. Through exploring stories like this, through such unshakeable belief and trust in a positive unfolding, we all can experience remarkable manifestations. These examples serve as inspiration and practical demonstrations of how unwavering faith can be a powerful substance in harnessing the flow of the universe for personal growth and manifestation.

***

In concluding this chapter, we've researched into the profound realm of believing in belief as a powerful tool to harness the flow of the universe.

The mantra's assertion, "And I know, like I know, like I know with unwavering faith that all this is happening for a reason, a good reason, actually it's a great reason," became our compass through the exploration of transformative beliefs.

We've witnessed how belief acts as a transformative force, shaping our perceptions and influencing the energetic currents of the universe. The repetition of the phrase "I know, like I know, Like I know," was unveiled as more than a verbal flourish—it's a deliberate reinforcement, a declaration of unwavering certainty that transcends doubt.

Through a personal example in my career journey, we've seen the profound impact of unwavering faith on manifestation. Hitting a rock bottom, losing everything, yet rising with unwavering faith, I not only recovered but soared to heights beyond previous achievements. My journey stands as a beacon, inspiring others to embrace unwavering faith in their pursuits.

As we navigated the concept of a "great reason" behind life events, we uncovered the importance of interpreting challenges as opportunities for growth. Embracing a positive reason behind every occurrence aligns us with the cosmic flow, pushing us toward our goals.

In essence, believing in belief is more than a mental exercise; it's a dynamic force that shapes the narrative of our lives. The mantra's affirmation isn't just a statement; it's a declaration that echoes in the massive span of the universe. As we move forward, let this unwavering faith be our guiding star, steering us through the cosmic currents toward the manifestation of our deepest aspirations. Let's stay tuned as we continue to unravel the layers of my mantra, exploring the intricacies of its sense in the chapters that follow.

We also discussed that while both approaches of harnessing the flow of the universe and going with the flow involve a profound acknowledgment of the cosmic forces shaping our existence, the decision to harness the flow or go with it hinges on individual inclinations, beliefs, and the context of one's life journey. The richness of human experience lies in the diversity of these perspectives, and individuals may find value in either approach at different points in their lives, creating a dynamic interplay between active engagement and serene acceptance on the ever-unfolding canvas of existence.

6 THE UNIVERSE'S RESPONSE

As we examined each part of the first half of the mantra so far, exploring the art of living in the present, cultivating feeling good, expressing gratitude, the power of affirmation, and deeply believing in the power of belief, it's now the moment of anticipation. The stage is set to witness the magnificent response of the universe to our intentional and harmonious engagement with its flow.

And as we seamlessly transition from our exploration of unwavering belief in the previous chapter, solidifying our understanding that every aspect of our lives unfolds for a great reason, we embark on the next leg of our cosmic journey. The mantra continues to unfold with a compelling affirmation, propelling us into a profound exploration: 'It's just the universe responding to the nature of my soul, to the song of my heart, and to my prayers.'

Here, we continue to believe that the universe's response to the essence of our being, attuning to the melodious vibrations emanating from our hearts. This chapter is an invitation to all of us to decode the cosmic echoes of our prayers. It serves as a gateway, opening a portal to grasp the profound connections that bind our conscious intentions to the universe's majestic response. Join us as we unravel the celestial symphony echoing our deliberate engagement with the ever-flowing energy of the cosmos, forging a deeper understanding of our cosmic interplay.

***

The Nature of My Soul:

In this exploration of the concept of the soul and its intrinsic relationship with the vast cosmos. There's a timeless philosophical and spiritual understanding of the soul, considering it as the eternal essence that exceeds physical existence.

There's a dynamic interplay between the authentic nature of the soul and the responsive nature of the universe. Here, we consider how authenticity, honesty, and alignment with one's true self create a harmonious echo with the cosmic energies.

The universe, with its endless intelligence, recognizes and responds to the genuine essence within us. And here, I would like to share with all of you a real-life example where I was able to employ the universe to illustrate the transformative power of embracing and expressing the authentic nature of my soul.

In a pivotal chapter of my career, I found myself navigating a challenging situation with a boss who seemingly held an unfathomable dislike towards me. The workplace environment became increasingly tense, with rumors circulating that my job was on the line. This supervisor, driven by motives I couldn't comprehend, appeared determined to find a pretext to terminate my employment.

Amidst the uncertainty, I chose to anchor myself in the authentic nature of my soul—a reservoir of honesty, integrity, and trust in the greater cosmic design. Instead of submitting to fear or taking defensive measures, I consciously relied on the belief that the universe would not allow harm to befall me without just cause.

I wasn't entirely passive during this challenging situation; however, my proactive approach was quite intriguing. Coincidentally, I had recently started exploring meditation, and in one session focused on managing anger, I learned a technique involving visualizing people with whom I had strained relationships and imagining them smiling and happy. Curiously, I began applying this practice to the specific issue with my boss, envisioning him in a positive light. At that time, I was somewhat naive, not realizing the potential miraculous impact this approach could have on my situation.

Miraculously, the universe responded in a way I hadn't anticipated. Through no direct action on my part, the truth about my boss's malicious intentions came to light. The universe orchestrated a series of events that exposed the plotting and ill intentions, ultimately leading to the dismissal of this boss rather than me.

This real-life example serves as a testament to the transformative power of embracing the authentic nature of the soul. By aligning with the innate goodness within and trusting the universe's inherent sense of justice, I not only weathered the storm but witnessed a profound cosmic response that safeguarded my well-being and integrity. This experience reinforced my understanding of the interconnected dance between the soul and the universe, affirming that authenticity and trust in the greater plan can lead to unexpected and positive outcomes.

***

The Song of My Heart:

The metaphorical use of the term "song" in the mantra, exploring its deeper meaning and significance, as if the heart's expression is likened to a song, reflecting the unique and authentic melody that radiates from within. By examining this metaphor, we aim to uncover the profound connection between the emotional echo within our hearts and the broader cosmic dance.

There is an amazing relationship between emotions, intentions, and the universe. The emotional landscape of our hearts, akin to a melody, reverberates through the cosmos, illuminate the ways in which our emotional states and intentions contribute to the vibrational energy that interacts with the universe, influencing its responsive dance.

***

My Prayers:

Regardless of one's religious or spiritual beliefs, prayers are profound messages sent out to the higher powers, whether it be God, the universe, the collective energy, or any force we hold in respect. In this part of our journey, we unravel the essence of prayer as a powerful form of intentional communication with the cosmic forces.

The prayers have a transformative power, exceeding religious boundaries. Prayers serve as intentional communication with the higher power. By examining the purposeful nature of prayers, we uncover their ability to transcend our beliefs and connect with the cosmic energies that shape our existence.

The consistent practice of prayer serves as a continuous dialogue with the higher power—be it God, the universe, or any divine force. As we engage in this ongoing communication, our messages echo in the massiveness of the cosmic realm. The more we invest in prayer, the more attentive the higher power becomes, actively listening and eventually responding to our intentions. In this reciprocal relationship, we emerge as co-creators of our lives, influencing our reality through the intentional and harmonious connection established by our prayers.

***

The Interconnected Dance:

As we learn together how to create, develop, and start reciting our mantra on daily basis to be able to harness the flow of the universe, we learn how to weave the threads of the soul's nature, the melody of the heart, prayers, and every other element explored in the mantra.

Through these different elements, we realize how they collaborate to influence the cosmic response. Even more, by examining their collective impact, we gain insights into the dynamic relationship between our intentional living and the way the universe responds to our energy.

In the comprehensive exploration of these diverse elements within our mantra, we uncover the collaborative cooperation that underlies their influence on the cosmic response. The essence of the soul, the melody of the heart, and the sincere prayers work in harmony, creating a unified vibrational frequency that echoes through the universe. This examination yields profound insights into the dynamic relationship between our intentional living practices and the nuanced way in which the universe understands and responds to the energy we emit.

The collective impact of these elements forms a harmonious tapestry, intricately woven with intention, emotion, and spiritual connection. It becomes a roadmap, a visual representation of our desires resonating with the universal flow. As we navigate this intricate tapestry, we discover that intentional living is not merely a solitary act but a collaborative dance with the cosmic forces, where each element within our mantra plays a unique and essential role.

***

Harnessing the Flow of the Universe and Going with the Flow:

Before we go any further, it's imperative to discuss the understated yet significant distinctions between harnessing the flow of the universe and going with the flow. Through recognizing this difference, we unveil two distinct models of engaging with the cosmic forces that shape our existence.

At the core of both concepts lies an acknowledgment of the larger cosmic forces at play, but their different paths become evident when examining the distinctions of active participation versus passive surrender, conscious direction versus adaptive acceptance, and purposeful alignment versus spontaneous responsiveness.

When we speak of harnessing the flow of the universe, there is a fundamental effect of active engagement and intentional direction. This approach is characterized by an active involvement in the cosmic energies, a conscious effort to direct these forces towards specific goals, and a purposeful alignment with the universal flow. It involves a recognition that personal actions can influence and shape the cosmic currents, and individuals actively participate in co-creating their reality.

Conversely, going with the flow represents a more passive, accepting, and adaptive stance towards the cosmic forces. This approach is characterized by a willingness to surrender to the natural rhythm of life without attempting to manipulate or control it actively. There is a deep acceptance of the present moment, a trust that the unfolding events are part of a larger, caring order, and an emphasis on adaptability and spontaneity in response to the ever-changing circumstances.

The choice between harnessing the flow and going with the flow ultimately depends on our philosophical orientation, goals, and the specific circumstances we encounter in life. Those who resonate with the idea of active creation, intentional direction, and purposeful alignment may find harnessing the flow more appealing. It aligns with a worldview that sees individuals as conscious contributors to their reality, shaping outcomes through deliberate engagement with cosmic energies.

On the other hand, those who prioritize acceptance, adaptability, and a more passive role in the grand scheme of things may resonate with going with the flow. This approach suits individuals who find value in embracing the spontaneity of life, living in the present moment, and navigating the unpredictable nature of existence with equanimity.

7 THE POWER OF ASKING

In this crucial chapter, we discuss the transformative force inherent in the act of asking. The power of asking serves as a crucial catalyst in our journey to harness the flow of the universe. By understanding the significance of vocalizing our desires, we unlock the potential to shape our reality and manifest our aspirations. This section is a profound exploration into the art of expressing our wants and needs with clarity and intention.

As we continue analyzing the layers of my own mantra, the subject of asking emerges as a cornerstone in our intentional engagement with the cosmic energies. The mantra's evolution parallels our growing understanding of how the universe responds to our thoughts, feelings, and explicit requests. The power of asking links seamlessly with the wider narrative of our cosmic journey, providing a key element in the dance of manifestation.

Within the mantra, a thoughtful part unfolds: "The universe is rearranging itself for me right now to give me exactly what I want. And what I want is: ...., ..., ..., ..., ..."

Quick disclaimer: it's important to note that the deliberate exclusion of my personal goals and desires from the mantra stems from a consideration of privacy. This intentional omission also carries a larger significance—it highlights the mantra's characteristic flexibility and adaptability.

The mantra is not a static entity but a dynamic tool that can be tailored to suit individual needs and preferences. It's a reminder that our lives are ever evolving, marked by changing circumstances, experiences, and aspirations. As we journey through life and our desires undergo transformation, the mantra can seamlessly evolve with us, staying in harmony with the flow of our personal narratives.

***

The Essence of Asking:

The profound importance of asking for what we want is a fundamental aspect of intentional living. Asking serves as a dynamic force that drives us forward in our journey to manifest our desires. It indicates an active engagement with the universe, a declaration of our needs and aspirations. By unpacking the significance of this simple yet powerful act, we unravel the potential it holds in shaping our reality.

Asking is not merely a transactional request; rather, it's a profound dialogue with the cosmos. It involves a conscious expression of our desires, creating a vibrational significance that waves through the universe. Understanding the depth of this exchange lays the foundation for a transformative relationship with the energies around us.

Furthermore, we recognize the fundamental role of intention. Asking with intention goes beyond mere words; it involves filling our requests with a deep sense of purpose and authenticity. Clarity and intention harmonize, creating a powerful combination that enhances the vibrational quality of our asks.

To bring these concepts to life, I will share with you a real-life example that illustrate the transformative impact of expressing desires through asking.

While I intentionally chose not to disclose specific personal desires in the earlier presentation of my mantra, I'm now willing to share one to illuminate the practical application of the power of asking. Among my current goals, consistently recited in my daily mantra, is the aspiration to continue traveling the world.

A few years ago, my wife and I created a vivid and inspiring vision board. Together, we carefully selected and posted images of all the breathtaking destinations we had longed to visit.

This vision board became more than just a collection; it evolved into a powerful tool for manifesting our dreams. Visualization became our language to communicate with the universe, a way to express our desires and aspirations.

When reciting my mantra, I took intentional steps to name each destination, detailing the order in which we wished for them to materialize in our reality.

Remarkably, my wife and I have experienced a substantial increase in our travels to new destinations. What's even more fascinating is that we find ourselves exploring places we hadn't even considered before—they simply come across our path.

This example serves as undeniable narrative, showcasing how the act of asking, when filled with clarity and intention, becomes a catalyst for manifestation. Whether in personal relationships, career aspirations, or broader life goals, the transformative power of expressing desires becomes evident through these stories. They inspire a deeper understanding of the profound connection between articulating our wants and the universe's responsive dance.

***

Missing Opportunities without Asking:
In the choreography between our aspirations and the universe's response, the influence of silence emerges as a potential obstruction. When we choose not to express our desires clearly, we

unintentionally create a barrier that can obstruct the actualization of our goals and dreams.

The consequences of such silence extend far beyond the mere missing of opportunities; they connect with the very essence of our existence. By refraining from vocalizing our aspirations, we unintentionally send to the universe a sense of satisfaction with the current state of affairs. This unintentional communication has the potential to disrupt the natural flow of energies eagerly poised to align with our intentions.

Therefore, it becomes imperative for us to break free from the state of silence and actively engage in clear communication with the universe. We even can consider the universe as a catalog to encourages us to actively communicate our desires.

***

The Universal Catalogue:

Consider the universe as a spacious catalogue, brimming with infinite possibilities waiting to be explored. In this metaphorical idea of treating the cosmos as a cosmic marketplace, our desires and aspirations are the items on display. By introducing the concept of the universe as a catalogue, we invite a shift in perspective—one that encourages us to actively engage with the abundant offerings available to us. This metaphor serves as a powerful visualization tool, helping us navigate the vast array of experiences, relationships, and possessions that the universe presents to us.

As we examine the cosmic catalogue, we realize that the universe is not a passive supplier but a dynamic collaborator. The power lies in our ability to distinguish and select, much like a savvy shopper browsing through a catalogue of life's offerings. By consciously selecting the experiences, relationships, and possessions we desire, we tap into the transformative potential of intentional living. The cosmic catalogue is vast, and our ability to choose becomes a beacon guiding us toward the fulfillment of our deepest aspirations.

***

Believing in the Rearrangement:

As we explore the nature of belief, we discover its crucial role in enhancing the transformative power of our intentional requests to the universe. This part sheds light on the influential strength of strong and unwavering belief, acting as an amplifier in the cosmic rearrangement process. Our belief serves as a magnetic force, bringing the cosmic dance closer to turning our heartfelt desires into reality.

Picture belief like a supportive breeze guiding our cosmic journey—a motivating force moving us ahead in the dance of rearrangement. As we explore the extensive cosmic catalog, selecting experiences, relationships, and possessions, unwavering belief becomes a subtle force strengthening the cosmic currents, speeding up the fulfillment of our intentional requests. It's a unwavering confidence that the universe, in its boundless wisdom, is not just responding but actively adjusting itself to harmonize with the tunes of our heartfelt desires.

In simple terms, belief goes beyond just watching; it becomes a key player, shaping the core of our reality. By intentionally connecting with cosmic forces and maintaining unwavering belief, we step into the role of co-creators in the cosmic symphony. Each time we repeat our mantra, we sync with the cosmic beat, directing the smooth rearrangement of our lives.

***

In wrapping up this chapter about the strong impact of asking in our mantra, let's think about how powerful this intentional act can be. Imagine the universe as a big store full of possibilities, just waiting for us to actively and purposefully explore what it has to offer.

In the intentional dance of living, asking is a sacred and proactive step, expressing our desires to the cosmos. Envision the universe as a responsive partner, always ready to rearrange itself to fulfill our wishes. It's not a passive interaction but an active collaboration where we, as conscious creators, choose from the cosmic array.

As we express our desires in the mantra, we have rooted trust in the universe. We believe in the rearrangement effect, in cosmic forces aligning to fulfill our deepest wishes. This trust is the catalyst driving the manifestation process, guiding us as we choose experiences, relationships, and possessions that resonate with our essence.

The beauty is in both asking and holding unwavering faith. As we repeat our requests, we build the belief that the universe responds to our intentional asks in its massive cosmic catalogue. It's a harmonious exchange, a cosmic dialogue where we express, and the universe rearranges itself to fulfill.

As we live intentionally by asking, let's bring this awareness to our daily recitations. Let's have faith in the universe's rearranging power, enjoy the dance between our desires and cosmic responses. The cosmic catalogue is vast, and our intentional choices unlock its treasures. May our aspirations harmonize with the cosmic symphony, weaving a life filled with our deepest desires.

8 VISUALIZATION

Stepping away momentarily from our detailed analysis of the mantra, let's examine the transformative practice of Visualization. During this brief pause, we will explore the powerful influence of mental imagery on shaping and molding our lived reality.

In this chapter, we uncover the deep connection between visualization and tapping into the universe's endless flow. In this chapter, we introduce the importance of visualization in intentional living. Going beyond the words of the mantra, we acknowledge the silent but impactful role of mental imagery. Envisioning our desires becomes a guiding force, deepening our connection with the universe.

***

Defining Visualization and Its Significance:

Visualization is the art of creating vivid mental images, a powerful tool that exceeds plain imagination. It involves vividly picturing our desires, dreams, and aspirations in our mind. The significance lies in its ability to translate these mental images into the fabric of our reality. Visualization acts as the bridge between the unearthly realm of thoughts and the tangible world, serving as a powerful spark in the manifestation process.

The role of mental imagery in intentional living is profound. It acts as the blueprint, the visual representation of what we wish to bring into our life. By vividly imagining our goals, we send clear signals to the universe, aligning our thoughts with our desires. Visualization becomes the originator to manifestation, shaping the energetic blueprint that the cosmic forces respond to. It's the intentional act of creating a mental movie where we are the protagonist, scripting the life we aspire to live.

Imagination is the designer of our reality. As we explore the power of visualization, we tap into the limitless potential of our creative minds. The ability to vividly imagine scenarios, experiences, and achievements opens the door to endless possibilities.

✳✳✳

Integrating Visualization Into our Mantra:

The blending of visualization with our mantra recitation elevates the practice to a new dimension. As we engage in uttering of our mantra, let's invite mental imagery to join the cosmic dance. Let's picture our desires, goals, and affirmations with vivid clarity. Integrate this visual layer into the recitation routine, transforming it into a full experience that engages not only the spoken words but also the vibrant images our mind conjures.

Visualization becomes the amplifier of our mantra's effectiveness. As we recite each word, we breathe life into the mental images associated with our intentions. We feel the emotions, we see the scenarios, and we embrace the experiences we desire. The marriage of spoken words and visualized intentions intensifies the energetic resonance, sending out a more potent frequency to the universe.

***

Techniques for Effective Visualization:

Practicality is crucial in seamlessly integrating visualization into your mantra recitation. Here are practical tips to effortlessly incorporate mental imagery during your recitation:

- Craft a Mental Vision Board: Within our mind's eye, envision images representing your aspirations, goals, and desires.

- Associate Visuals with Mantra Phrases: Assign specific visuals to each phrase of your mantra. For instance, if our mantra involves themes of abundance, visualize a garden blooming with vibrant flowers or vegetables as you recite. By linking visual cues to the words, we enhance the resonance of our intentions.

- Engage Multiple Senses: Amplify our mental imagery by engaging multiple senses. Feel the textures, smell the scents, and hear the sounds associated with your visualizations. This multisensory approach deepens the connection between your intentions and the cosmic energies.

- Build a Ritual Around Visualization: Establish a ritual that signals your mind to transition into visualization mode during mantra recitation. This could be a simple gesture, a deep breath, or a moment of stillness.

- Practice Mindful Visualization: Cultivate mindfulness as you visualize. Be fully present in the mental images, allowing them to unfold with clarity and detail. Mindful visualization enhances the effectiveness of your mantra recitation by fostering a deeper connection between your thoughts and the cosmic energies.

- Adapt Techniques to Your Style: Tailor these tips to suit your personal style and preferences. Experiment with different techniques and adopt the ones that resonate most with you. Making the process uniquely yours ensures that visualization seamlessly integrates into your daily recitation routine.

By combining these practical tips, we fill our mantra recitation with the dynamic energy of visualization, creating a harmonious interplay between spoken words and vivid mental imagery. This practical approach enhances the effectiveness of our intentional living practices, allowing us to harness the flow of the universe with ease.

***

The Science Behind Visualization:

Studying the science of visualization reveals how our minds connect with the process of bringing our desires into reality. Psychologically, visualization engages the brain's ability to create mental images, using the same neural networks as when processing real experiences. Neurologically, research suggests the brain may not consistently differentiate between vividly imagined scenes and real events. This lack of distinction emphasizes how powerful visualization can be in influencing how we perceive and respond to the world.

The subconscious mind, filled with beliefs and attitudes, greatly influences our actions and experiences. Visualization serves as a direct link to the subconscious. When we consistently expose our minds to positive mental images during mantra recitation, we imprint our desires on the subconscious. This repetition creates a connection, slowly aligning the subconscious with our conscious intentions. Consequently, the subconscious becomes a partner in guiding our actions toward manifesting our aspirations.

The connection between thoughts, emotions, and visualization is crucial for intentional living. Thoughts create mental images, which then arouse emotions. When positive emotions are combined with intentional images during visualization, they create a harmonious frequency that aligns with the universe's energy. This interconnected web of thoughts and emotions, fueled by visualization, impacts our energetic connection with the cosmic flow. Aligning positive thoughts and emotions boosts the manifestation process, strengthening the belief that our desires are not just achievable but already in motion within the cosmic dance.

Understanding the science behind visualization empowers us to use this tool consciously in intentional living. By delving into the psychological and neurological aspects, acknowledging the impact on the subconscious mind, and recognizing the dance between thoughts, emotions, and visualization, we grasp the transformative potential of this practice. Visualization becomes more than a creative effort; it becomes a scientifically supported method to harness the universe's flow and manifest our deepest desires.

***

Allow me to share a personal story about the remarkable impact of visualization on achieving my dreams. One potent approach I employed was the creation of vision boards, a tool for visualizing my goals. What may surprise you is that the examples I'll share are unintentional manifestations, emphasizing the effectiveness of visualization even when not openly intentional. These experiences serve as compelling evidence of the tangible results that can emerge through the power of visualization.

A few years ago, my wife and I embarked on a transformative journey by creating our own vision board. This visually compelling collection was adorned with many dreams—traveling the world, embracing wealth, fostering good health, and collecting a multitude of unique experiences. As we hung our aspirations on the board, little did we realize the profound impact it would have on our lives.

Remarkably, many of our dreams have already materialized, but what truly astonished us were the unintentional manifestations. Among the pictures that we included without fully comprehending its significance was one depicting a joyous lady immersed in what seemed to be a mud bath. At that moment, we were drawn to the sheer happiness radiating from her.

Fast forward a couple of years, and life unfolded in a way that took me by surprise. Unintentionally, I found myself in the picturesque volcanic mud baths of Cartagena, Colombia.

It wasn't until I returned home and shared the pictures from my solo vacation with my wife that something extraordinary unfolded. She drew my attention to an unintentional manifestation—I had experienced something that had been on our vision board for a couple of years. As we went through the photos, my wife pointed out that the location in one of the pictures perfectly matched a long-held aspiration we had pinned on our vision board. The joy I experienced even mirrored that of the lady in the image, if not surpassing it. This unexpected moment beautifully showcased the power of intentional living and how our visualizations can manifest in unexpected ways.

This unexpected encounter with our vision board reinforced the incredible power of visualization. It demonstrated that the images we had casually chosen, without fully understanding their implications, had become tangible realities in our lives. The mud bath adventure served as a touching reminder that the universe orchestrates its dance in mysterious ways, responding to our visualized dreams and bringing them to fruition in the most unexpected yet delightful manner.

Another compelling demonstration of the influence of visualization in harnessing the flow of the universe is found in my use of drawing as an effective tool for manifestation. Beyond the creation of a traditional vision board, I extend the reach of my intentions by leveraging my modest drawing skills to illustrate my dreams. Through the act of passionately expressing my desires on paper, I hold the belief that the communication with the universe becomes more immediate, precise, and impactful.

To facilitate this practice, I always maintain a simple drawing kit and a small pad within arm's reach, allowing me to spontaneously and consistently sketch my dreams as they unfold in my mind. Remarkably, the universe has responded in kind by transforming these illustrations into tangible reality. Whether it's materializing travel plans to specific destinations, achieving significant career milestones, experiencing the joys of romance, cultivating meaningful personal relationships, or reaching financial goals, the act of drawing has evolved into a profound and effective means of co-creating with the cosmic energies. This personal example highlights the transformative potential of intentional visualization in shaping and manifesting the desired aspects of our reality.

***

In wrapping up our study of visualization in intentional living, let's capture the main ideas from this chapter. Visualization, whether through vision boards or mental imagery, stands out as a powerful force shaping our reality. It involves infusing our intentions with vivid mental images, actively engaging in the cosmic dance to align our desires with the universe's energy.

We've explored how visualization influences our subconscious mind, becoming a transformative tool that communicates with our beliefs. Through intentional practice, we imprint our desires on the subconscious, making it a co-pilot in steering our actions towards what we want.

Our dive into the science behind visualization highlights its impact on thoughts, emotions, and the manifestation process. By recognizing the connection between positive thoughts, emotions, and visualization, we strengthen our alignment with the cosmic flow, reinforcing the belief that our desires are already unfolding within the cosmic symphony.

Understanding the science behind visualization empowers us to use this tool consciously in intentional living. We've seen how it connects with the overarching theme of harnessing the flow of the universe, forming a synergistic relationship with the mantra breakdown. The upcoming chapters promise deeper insights into intentional living, unlocking more secrets to navigate the vast cosmic dance. Join us as we explore further layers of the mantra, stepping into the rhythm of intentional living, co-creating our reality within the grand tapestry of existence.

9 THE MIRACLE

At the apex of our thoughtful journey through the mantra, we encounter the final lines resonating with unwavering faith in the looming miracle: "And I know, like I know, like I know with unwavering faith that this is all happening for me right now, and that I'm pulling off a miracle, the miracle of harnessing the flow of the universe. Amen and thank you."

In this chapter, we embark on an in-depth exploration of the triple affirmation, the unwavering faith, the ability to pull off miracles, and the transformative force of gratitude in the finale. Each element serves as a key pillar in our intentional symphony, contributing to the resonance and manifestation of our desires.

***

The Triple Affirmation:

As we discussed un the previous chapters, the repetition of "I know, like I know, like I know" within the mantra is similar to a holy chant, resonating with a profound power that exceeds the realm of mere belief. This repetition serves as a mantra within the larger affirmation, acting as a focal point that amplifies the intensity of the message. It goes beyond the surface level of belief and enters the domain of deep, unshakable knowing.

The choice of words, particularly the emphatic "I know," highlights a level of certainty that is unwavering and resolute. This is not a passive acknowledgment or a hopeful emotion; it is a declaration of absolute assurance. The repetition further emphasizes the intensity of this knowing, creating a rhythm that reverberates through the consciousness.

This knowing is not grounded in logical reasoning alone; it is steeped in unwavering faith. It is a trust that extends beyond the tangible, beyond what can be seen or proven in conventional terms. This faith becomes the foundation upon which the entire affirmation stands. It is the solid foundation upon which the intentional symphony is orchestrated.

Unwavering faith, in this context, is not a momentary feeling but a steady, shining force. It is a belief in the alignment of cosmic forces, a trust that the universe is conspiring to bring forth the deepest desires. This faith becomes a guiding light in the intentional journey, providing stability and confidence amidst the ebb and flow of life.

In essence, the repetition of "I know, like I know, like I know" serves as a transformative tool, driving us into a state of deep knowing and unwavering faith. It acts as a beacon in the intentional symphony, harmonizing the vibrations of belief, trust, and certainty to manifest the desired outcomes in the cosmic dance of existence.

***

With Unwavering Faith:

This phrase functions as a vital bridge, seamlessly connecting the realm of knowing to the unfolding reality in the intentional symphony. This phrase symbolizes a profound acknowledgment, signaling the recognition that the faith being referred to is not a flickering flame open to external winds but rather a steady, luminous beacon that persistently guides the way through the cosmic dance of existence.

The adjective "unwavering" is deliberate and carries substantial weight, emphasizing the firm and unyielding nature of this faith. It stands tall against doubts and uncertainties, remaining constant even in the face of challenges. This unwavering quality transforms faith into a reliable guide, a source of strength that endures throughout the intentional journey.

The phrase summarizes a profound trust in the cosmic forces at play. It goes beyond a mere belief; it is a recognition and surrender to the web of energies conspiring to manifest the deepest desires. This trust is rooted in the understanding that the universe operates with a certain order and purpose, and with unwavering faith, one aligns themselves with this cosmic choreography.

The alignment of energies, mentioned in the phrase, signifies a harmonious cooperation between our intentions and the universal forces. It's a recognition that intentional living is not a isolated work but a collaborative dance with the cosmos. "With unwavering faith" becomes a mantra that ushers us into this harmonious dance, instilling confidence and reliance on the orchestrated alignment of cosmic energies.

***

Pulling Off Miracles:

This expression places the concept of pulling off a miracle at the front, inviting us to dig into its layers and untangle the profound connection between intentional living and the extraordinary.

The phrase "pulling off a miracle" implies a transformative and exceptional outcome, one that exceeds normal expectations. In the context of intentional living, it suggests that through deliberate practices and alignment with cosmic energies, we can manifest outcomes that might be perceived as extraordinary or even miraculous.

Before we go any further, let's explore a real-life narrative illustrating the concept of pulling off miracles through intentional living and harnessing the flow of the universe:

187

My wife, Karen, with nearly three decades of managerial experience in the hospitality industry, found herself at a crossroads, yearning to turn her lifelong dream of becoming a successful real estate agent into a reality. Despite facing numerous challenges in a highly competitive market, Karen made the courageous decision to leap from her familiar role in hospitality to intentionally manifest her aspirations.

Key to Karen's intentional living approach was her unwavering faith in the abundance of the universe. Recognizing the importance of maintaining positivity amid initial setbacks and obstacles, she anchored herself in the belief that cosmic forces were actively conspiring to support her vision. In moments of uncertainty, Karen turned to affirmations, using them as tools to reaffirm her faith and vividly visualize the miraculous success she aspired to achieve.

As Karen consistently engaged in intentional practices, remarkable events began to unfold. Unexpected opportunities presented themselves—a prominent business mentor extended valuable guidance, a pivotal partnership emerged, and her real estate services garnered positive reviews from satisfied clients. These synchronicities, akin to miracles, perfectly aligned with the intentional energy Karen had infused into her daily practices.

The pinnacle of Karen's intentional living journey manifested in the successful launch and rapid growth of her real estate business. What initially seemed like an ambitious dream excelled into a reality that surpassed even Karen's initial expectations. Beyond her success as a real estate agent, Karen emerged as a respected and influential figure within the broader real estate community, poised on the brink of achieving the esteemed status of a broker.

Karen's entrepreneurial triumph stands as a powerful witness to the transformative potential of intentional living in pulling off miracles. By consciously aligning her thoughts, words, and actions with the cosmic dance, she manifested a business success that defied conventional odds—an inspiring example of harnessing the flow of the universe to bring about miraculous results.

***

Gratitude Finale:

As we approach the grand finale of our intentional symphony, the spotlight turns towards the profound significance encapsulated in the concluding line: "Amen and thank you." This crucial section aims to unravel the transformative power embedded in the practice of gratitude, positioning it as the concluding note in our intentional living journey.

The term "Amen" is traditionally used to affirm or conclude prayers. In the realm of intentional living, "Amen" becomes a powerful acknowledgment of the faith and certainty with which we navigate our journey.

Moving to the second part, "thank you" becomes the focal point. Gratitude is celebrated as the finale of our intentional symphony, acknowledging the abundance that flows through the cosmic dance. The transformative power of gratitude is explored in depth, shedding light on its ability to shape our perception, attitude, and energetic resonance with the universe.

In essence, "Gratitude Finale: Amen and Thank You" serves as a powerful conclusion to our intentional journey, inviting readers to recognize the transformative potential embedded in the simple yet profound act of expressing gratitude. Through reflections, practices, and stories, this section seeks to inspire a lasting sense of appreciation, fostering a harmonious connection with the cosmic symphony.

***

In conclusion, the final lines of the mantra represent a peak of unwavering faith, miraculous manifestation, and profound gratitude. These affirmations, encapsulated in the words "And I know, like I know, like I know with unwavering faith that this is all happening for me right now, and that I'm pulling off a miracle, the miracle of harnessing the flow of the universe. Amen and thank you," serve as the climax in our intentional symphony.

The repetition of "I know, like I know, like I know" within these lines acts as a powerful mantra within the mantra, underscoring a level of certainty that exceeds plain belief. It signifies a deep, unshakable knowing steeped in unwavering faith—an acknowledgment that goes beyond the realm of doubt. This profound knowing becomes the foundation upon which the entire affirmation stands, guiding us through the cosmic dance.

"With unwavering faith" serves as a bridge between knowing and the unfolding reality. It signifies an acknowledgment that this faith is not a wavering flame but a steady, luminous beacon guiding the way through the cosmic dance. It summarizes a trust in the cosmic forces, a trust in the alignment of energies conspiring to manifest our deepest desires.

The concept of pulling off a miracle takes center stage as we analyze its layers. This involves a journey through personal stories and practical insights, unveiling the collaboration between intentional manifestation and the seemingly extraordinary results that unfold. The intentional living journey becomes a deliberate act of co-creation with the cosmic forces, where our thoughts, words, and actions align harmoniously to usher in the miraculous.

Approaching the grand finale, we shine a spotlight on the significance of concluding with "Amen and thank you." Gratitude becomes the concluding note in our intentional symphony, emphasizing its transformative power. This section delves into tangible ways to infuse gratitude into our daily intentional practices, recognizing it as a dynamic force that amplifies intentional vibrations within the cosmic dance.

As we navigate the cosmic dance, these final lines of the mantra serve as a guiding light, inspiring us to embrace the miracles that unfold when we align our intentions with the boundless flow of the universe. "Amen and thank you" becomes a heartfelt expression, acknowledging the journey of intentional living with deep gratitude. It is an affirmation that resonates with the universe, signaling the end of one phase and the beginning of another—a harmonious conclusion to our intentional symphony.

10 POSITIVE THOUGHT AND SPEECH

As we look back on our intentional living journey, we've closely examined the mantra, exploring the deep links between words, thoughts, and the cosmic dance. Now, at this crucial point in our intentional symphony, we move beyond the recurring recitation of the mantra to every moment of our daily life—controlling our thoughts and words deliberately.

This chapter acts as a guide, providing insights into observing, refining, and mastering our inner and outer dialogue. Its aim is to empower us, ensuring that our internal and external stories align smoothly with the vast cosmic forces shaping our reality. Through this transformative practice, we navigate the landscape of intentional living, understanding that our thoughts and words have the ability to influence and co-create with the expansive energies of the universe.

***

The Power of Thought and Speech:

At the heart of intentional living lies the remarkable power characteristic in our thoughts and words. Far beyond being mere expressions, they emerge as vibrant energies endowed with the profound capability to mold and shape our reality. The all-encompassing wisdom of the universe is strongly adapted to the involved vibrations we produce into the cosmos. Similar to the mantra, which acts as a sacred conduit for intentional living, our daily thoughts and words stand as formidable compounds, serving to drive us consistently towards the materialization of our most cherished dreams.

In the essence of this understanding, the energy embedded within our thoughts and words takes on the role of a dynamic force. It actively links with the cosmic dance, becoming an essential part of the symphony of intentional living. Through this dynamic relationship, our thoughts and words become active participants in shaping the course of our intentional living journey, infusing it with the enthusiasm needed for the manifestation of our deepest aspirations.

***

Monitoring Our Thoughts and Words:

To tap into the vast flow of the universe, a fundamental step is keeping a close eye on our inner and external dialogue. This means paying attention to the stories we tell ourselves within our minds and the words coming out of our mouths. Are our thoughts and words consistently positive, or do they often lean towards doubt and negativity?

Monitoring our inner and external dialogue requires a conscious and deliberate approach. It involves staying aware of the thoughts crossing our minds and words we utter moment by moment. Through this mindful observation, we uncover patterns and recognize the sensitive differences in our self-talk and conversations with others. This increased self-awareness serves as a powerful tool, helping us determine whether our thoughts align with the harmonious vibrations of the cosmic dance or veer into dissonance.

By being mindful of our inner dialogue and the words we utter, we embrace intentional living. Actively examining our thoughts and words allows us to enhance and reshape the stories we create within ourselves and around us, making sure they resonate with positivity, purpose, and harmony with the vast energies of the universe. This journey of monitoring our thoughts and words is transformative, guiding us towards intentional alignment and co-creation with the cosmic symphony.

***

Adapting to Positive Patterns:

Upon identifying the recurring patterns within our thoughts and words, the subsequent stage in our intentional living journey involves a purposeful act of adaptation. This transformative process empowers us to shift our internal dialogue and our conversations with others from the realm of self-doubt to one characterized by unwavering belief and positivity. It is a dynamic dance of conscious choice, where we recognize the effectiveness of our thoughts and words in shaping our reality and take intentional steps to redefine the narrative.

Adapting to positive patterns requires a deliberate effort to replace negative thoughts and words with affirmations rooted in optimism and empowerment. It is a conscious decision to redirect the course of our internal dialogue, cultivating a mindset that acts as a magnet for abundance and fulfillment. In this process of adaptation, we become architects of our own mental landscape, constructing a foundation built on positivity, resilience, and a deep knowing that aligns with the cosmic dance.

The journey of intentional living involves not only recognizing the need for change but actively participating in the transformation of our thought and word patterns. Through this adaptation, we harness the creative power of our minds, co-creating a reality that resonates with the harmonious vibrations of the universe. As we consciously shape our internal dialogue and the words we say, we step into the role of intentional architects, designing a mental blueprint that aligns with our aspirations and the expansive energies of the cosmic symphony.

***

Dominating with Optimism:

Choosing optimism is a crucial step in living with intention, recognizing how our thoughts and words shape our reality. The universe responds to the positive vibes we generate internally. Being optimistic doesn't mean ignoring real emotions or challenges but involves consciously adopting empowering perspectives. By focusing on constructive and positive narratives, we actively shape our reality within the vast cosmic dance.

Our thoughts and words produce energies that communicate with the universe, and when optimism dominates our internal and external dialogue, it creates harmony with cosmic forces. This proactive engagement aligns our intentions with the abundance and creative flow of the cosmos.

Dominating with optimism means seeing challenges as opportunities, setbacks as steppingstones, and uncertainties as gateways to growth. It's about acknowledging life's ups and downs while deliberately focusing on the positive.

***

The Universe as an Active Listener:

In intentional living, the idea of the universe as an active listener is crucial. This concept highlights how our thoughts, words, and cosmic forces interact to shape our reality. It emphasizes the universe's dynamic, responsive nature and its active role in the intricate dance of existence.

Essentially, viewing the universe as an active listener means it's not passive but a dynamic force tuning into the vibrations from our thoughts and words. This idea aligns with energy and vibration principles, reflecting the interconnected dance that shapes the cosmic symphony.

Our thoughts and words are like energetic signals that connect with the universe. The universe actively listens and responds. When our thoughts are positive and aligned with our desires, the universe works with us to make our dreams come true. It becomes a partner, shaping events, aligning circumstances, and creating paths for our aspirations to come to life.

On the flip side, if our thoughts are negative or doubtful, the universe acts like a mirror, reflecting these discordant signals. This disrupts the harmony in the cosmic dance, and obstacles may arise in the manifestation process. It highlights how important our conscious choices are in shaping the vibrations we send into the cosmos.

Seeing the universe as an active listener reminds us that we play a role in creating our reality. Actively participating in the dance of creation involves cultivating positive thoughts, showing gratitude, and aligning our intentions with the cosmic flow. The universe, like a responsive partner, listens to our dominant frequencies and reflects them in our manifested experiences.

***

Exploring how we control our thoughts and words reveals a profound aspect of intentional living that goes beyond mere mantra repetition. Intentional living is a complete journey involving careful cultivation of our inner world—a continuous dance aligning our thoughts and words with the universal rhythm.

Mastering intentional living recognizes the crucial role our internal dialogue plays in shaping reality. It's not just about what we say or think but a conscious collaboration with cosmic forces governing existence's grand symphony. This journey requires heightened awareness, mindful presence, navigating our thoughts, and expressing the energy in our words.

Engaging in this intentional dance elevates us to conscious co-creators, actively shaping our reality rather than passively navigating life. Our thoughts become brushstrokes, and our words, melodies, creating a vibrant tapestry of our deepest aspirations. Continuously refining our inner dialogue to match universal frequencies is part of the process.

Stepping into the symphony of existence, let our thoughts and words harmonize with the cosmic dance, infusing intentionality into every aspect of our being. This is an invitation to align aspirations with the cosmic flow, manifesting with resonance through the intricate threads of existence.

Dominating our thoughts and words is an art of conscious living—a dynamic practice transforming our inner world and shaping the reality we experience. Through this intentional dance, we forge a harmonious connection with cosmic forces, co-creating a life actively manifested in collaboration with the universe's boundless abundance.

FINAL MESSAGE

As we conclude our journey through the exploration of harnessing the flow of the universe, let's carry with us a timeless reminder: always hold onto hope, embrace your strength, wear a smile as a constant companion, let laughter resonate loudly, play with unwavering enthusiasm, savor the beauty of each moment, dream big with boundless ambition, and above all, choose happiness as your guiding star.

***

Hope is like a guiding light in the journey of life, helping us navigate through its twists and turns. It acts as a steady compass, especially during challenging and uncertain times. Life is full of unexpected challenges, but hope is a reliable companion that provides direction and purpose. It empowers us to face obstacles with courage, believing in a brighter tomorrow even in the face of hardship.

In moments of uncertainty, hope keeps us grounded like an anchor. It encourages us to focus on possibilities, seeing challenges as steppingstones rather than challenging barriers. Hope allows us to embrace the journey with anticipation, sustaining us in the present while paving the way for a promising future.

Hope is not just a personal force but a communal one that brings people together. Shared among individuals, it creates a collective strength that transcends individual struggles, fostering unity and mutual support. Holding onto hope reminds us that we are not alone on this journey.

In essence, hope is a resilient force shaping our perspective and actions. By anchoring ourselves in hope, we acknowledge life's challenges but also embrace the transformative power of a positive outlook. It becomes a guiding light, turning challenges into opportunities and uncertainties into steppingstones on the journey of life.

***

Strength is a powerful force that helps us tackle life's challenges. It gives us resilience, determination, and a strong belief that we can overcome anything.

Embracing our inner strength means recognizing and using our resilience—the ability to bounce back from difficulties without giving up. It's a quiet but strong force that helps us endure tough times and come out stronger.

Determination, another aspect of strength, is the mental and emotional courage to keep going through challenges. It's the stamina that pushes us forward when things get tough, allowing us to navigate difficulties with a strong spirit.

Believing in our ability to overcome obstacles is a crucial part of inner strength. This belief, rooted in self-confidence, trusts our ability to find solutions and move forward. It turns challenges into chances for growth, seeing obstacles not as impossible barriers but as steps toward personal development.

Inner strength includes mental, emotional, and spiritual aspects, going beyond just physical abilities. It's about understanding our weaknesses but choosing to move forward with courage. It's a dynamic relationship between recognizing our limits and using the strength within us.

In tough times, strength guides us through challenges with calm determination, knowing that even in the darkest moments, there's an inner light to lead us forward.

Strength becomes a cornerstone of our character, shaping how we face life's challenges. It's a source of resilience, determination, and unwavering faith, forming the foundation to endure and thrive in hardship. By embracing our inner strength, we turn challenges into chances for personal growth and empowerment. It reminds us that within each person lies a vast reservoir of courage waiting to be discovered and used.

***

The simple yet profound act of wearing a smile emerges as a powerful force, uplifting not only our own spirits but creating a wave effect of positivity in our interactions with others.

At its core, smiling is more than a facial expression; it is a conscious choice to cultivate an optimistic and joyful demeanor. Choosing to wear a smile as a constant companion signifies a commitment to navigate through life's ups and downs with grace and positivity. It is a symbol of resilience, an acknowledgment that even in challenging moments, we possess the capacity to find joy.

The act of smiling triggers a waterfall of physiological and psychological benefits. Physiologically, it releases endorphins, our body's natural mood enhancers, creating a sense of well-being. Psychologically, smiling has the power to reduce stress and elevate our mood, contributing to a more positive outlook on life. By wearing a smile, we actively engage in a feedback loop that reinforces our emotional well-being.

Furthermore, a smile is a universal language that exceeds cultural and linguistic barriers. It serves as a non-verbal communication of warmth, approachability, and friendliness. When we wear a smile, we invite positive energy into our interactions, creating an atmosphere of openness and connection. A genuine smile is contagious, sparking a positive response from those around us and fostering a harmonious environment.

Wearing a smile as a constant companion not only influences our internal state but also impacts our external circumstances. It becomes a self-fulfilling prophecy, attracting positivity and kindness from others. As we radiate warmth through our smiles, we invite reciprocal positive energy, creating a ripple effect that extends beyond our immediate interactions.

Moreover, the act of smiling enhances our ability to cope with challenges. It provides a brief break, allowing us to approach difficulties with a lighter perspective. A smile acts as a silent affirmation that we can navigate through adversity with resilience and grace.

In social settings, a genuine smile fosters a sense of friendship and builds lasting connections. It breaks down barriers, making connections more enjoyable and meaningful. The positive energy generated by a smile contributes to a supportive and uplifting social atmosphere.

In conclusion, wearing a smile as a constant companion is an art of joyful living. It goes beyond a mere facial expression; it is a deliberate choice to infuse optimism into our daily experiences. By embracing the power of a smile, we not only uplift our own spirits but also contribute to a positive and harmonious world, creating a wave effect of joy and kindness in our interactions with others.

***

In our daily lives, laughter stands out as a powerful and uplifting force. Letting laughter ring out loudly acts as a strong remedy for stress, bringing joy and a sense of lightness into our everyday experiences.

Considered a universal language of happiness, laughter has a unique ability to cut through life's tensions and challenges. When faced with stress, pressures, or the difficulties of our routines, laughter becomes a liberating force, creating space for relief and renewal.

Physically, laughter triggers positive changes in our bodies. It releases endorphins, the body's natural feel-good chemicals, promoting an overall sense of well-being. Additionally, laughter reduces stress hormones, offering a natural and accessible way to ease the burdens of daily life.

Beyond its physical benefits, laughter deeply impacts our mental and emotional well-being. It acts as a release controller for built-up tension and a tool for breaking down barriers. Shared laughter promotes connection and friendship, forming bonds that go beyond the challenges we face.

Choosing to let laughter resonate loudly is a conscious decision to face difficulties with a light-hearted perspective. It shifts our focus from the seriousness of problems to the lightness of the moment, encouraging us to find humor even in tough situations. This shift not only makes challenges more manageable but also builds resilience by fostering an optimistic outlook.

As a source of joy, laughter contributes to positive memories and experiences. It enhances the quality of our relationships, creating lasting bonds and strengthening connections. Integrating laughter into our daily lives establishes an atmosphere where joy becomes a constant companion, making even routine activities more enjoyable.

In essence, laughter is not just a reaction; it's a deliberate choice to embrace joy and lightness. Allowing laughter to resonate loudly becomes a transformative practice, enhancing our overall well-being, relieving stress, and fostering a positive atmosphere in our lives. Navigating life's complexities, the power of laughter remains a valuable ally, offering a refreshing and revitalizing perspective on our journey.

***

Play is a powerful force that nurtures inner joy, sparks creativity, and keeps a sense of wonder alive. Embracing life with enthusiasm and a playful spirit becomes a key to staying connected to the boundless joys within us.

Play, at its core, celebrates the liveliness of the human spirit, expressing creativity and inviting us to explore the world with childlike wonder. It's more than specific activities; it's a mindset that goes beyond the ordinary, tapping into the limitless possibilities surrounding us.

Approaching life with unwavering enthusiasm means filling every moment with a zest for exploration and discovery. It's about embracing each experience, even routine ones, with a fresh perspective. Enthusiasm is the spark that ignites curiosity, turning the ordinary into something extraordinary and transforming the ordinary into the magical.

A playful spirit extends beyond structured games; it's an attitude that shapes how we tackle challenges and opportunities. It involves openness, adaptability, and a willingness to take risks. In the realm of play, mistakes are not failures but steppingstones to learning and growth, fostering resilience and a positive outlook on life.

Play feeds our creativity, unlocking doors to innovation and new perspectives. It encourages thinking outside conventional boundaries, letting imagination solve problems and embrace fresh possibilities. By infusing a spirit of play into our endeavors, we tap into the wellspring of ingenuity within us, bringing novel ideas and insights to enrich our lives.

Moreover, a playful approach strengthens our connections with others. Shared moments of laughter, exploration, and creativity build bonds that go beyond surface-level interactions. Play becomes a universal language, fostering a sense of community and shared joy across ages, backgrounds, and differences.

In conclusion, play is a profound celebration of life's fundamental joy and a pathway to unlocking our fullest potential. It refreshes our spirits, keeps our creativity vibrant, and ensures we approach each day with wonder and anticipation. By embracing a playful spirit, we cultivate a reservoir of inner joy that not only enhances our lives but also radiates outward, creating a positive and uplifting impact on the world around us.

***

Living in the moment is a profound way to connect with the richness of unfolding experiences. It's a choice to recognize and enjoy the beauty in each moment, fostering mindfulness and gratitude that enhance our overall experience.

Living in the moment means intentionally being fully present, free from past distractions or future worries. It invites us to immerse ourselves in the current experience, letting physical details and emotions unfold without being cluttered by other thoughts. This mindfulness increases our awareness of the world and our own thoughts and feelings.

To savor the beauty of each moment, we need a shift in perspective—a conscious decision to appreciate simple joys and the little details in our daily lives. It involves finding the extraordinary in the ordinary, whether it's the warmth of sunlight, the rustle of leaves, or the laughter of a loved one. Focusing on the present enhances our ability to find joy in seemingly mundane aspects of life.

Mindfulness, a key part of living in the moment, involves observing thoughts and emotions without judgment. It encourages accepting the present as it is, fostering inner peace. Mindfulness allows us to respond to situations with clarity and intention, contributing to a balanced and centered way of living.

Gratitude naturally arises from living in the moment. As we tune into the beauty around us, we develop appreciation for the abundance in our lives. Gratitude acts as a powerful substance for joy, shifting our focus from what may be lacking to what we have, creating a positive and uplifting perspective.

In essence, living in the moment is an art that turns the ordinary into the extraordinary. It's a conscious embrace of the present, an invitation to cherish the beauty woven into each moment. Through this practice, we develop mindfulness, appreciate life's richness, and foster gratitude as a guiding light on our journey.

***

Dreaming big is a powerful force in life, encouraging us to nurture boundless ambition and explore endless possibilities. It involves setting ambitious goals, envisioning a future beyond current limitations, and adopting a mindset that transcends constraints. This practice acknowledges that our aspirations can go beyond the ordinary, inspiring, and challenging us.

Dreaming big is like igniting a powerful engine within us, driving our efforts with passion, creativity, and an unwavering commitment to pursuing our highest goals. It emphasizes that ambition, when unrestrained, propels us forward, even in the face of challenges. The size of the dream matters less than its potential impact on our lives and the world.

Cultivating boundless ambition means setting goals that stretch our abilities, pushing us beyond comfort zones. It involves embracing uncertainty and exploring uncharted territories of our potential. Dreaming big encourages breaking free from self-imposed limitations, fostering a mindset that views challenges as opportunities for growth rather than challenging obstacles.

Dreaming big is closely tied to passion and purpose, fueling our pursuits with a desire to make a meaningful impact beyond personal gain. A big dream becomes a source of inspiration, guiding our actions with a purpose that extends beyond individual aspirations, contributing to the collective progress of humanity.

Moreover, daring to dream big creates a ripple effect, inspiring others and fostering a culture of ambition and innovation. Sharing our big dreams becomes a substance for positive change, encouraging others to explore boundless possibilities in their own lives.

In essence, dreaming big celebrates human potential and commits to living a life of significance. It is a deliberate choice to unleash creativity, passion, and purpose, pushing us toward a future where possibilities are as vast as our imagination. By daring to dream big, we shape our destinies and contribute to a collective narrative of growth, inspiration, and the relentless pursuit of excellence.

***

Choosing happiness is a significant and transformative practice. Making happiness our guide has the power to align our intentions with the universal flow, creating a fulfilling and harmonious life.

Choosing happiness is more than a fleeting emotion; it's a conscious decision to approach life with positivity and optimism. It involves recognizing that, despite life's challenges, we have control over our perspective and responses.

By choosing happiness, we acknowledge our ability to shape the story of our lives.

Aligning our intentions with the universal flow is crucial in choosing happiness. It acknowledges the interconnected nature of all things and the dynamic forces in the cosmos. When we choose happiness consciously, our intentions sync with the expansive energy of the universe, guiding us toward a meaningful and satisfying life.

Choosing happiness doesn't mean ignoring genuine emotions or avoiding difficulties. Instead, it's a commitment to finding joy and gratitude even in challenging moments. It recognizes that happiness isn't solely tied to external circumstances but is significantly influenced by our internal dialogue and choices.

Choosing happiness is an active participation in shaping our reality. It involves creating a positive narrative, fostering an optimistic mindset that influences our daily interactions and relationships, enhancing overall well-being.

Moreover, choosing happiness extends beyond personal fulfillment; it contributes to the collective well-being of the universe. The positivity and joy we cultivate have a wave effect, inspiring and uplifting those around us, creating a connected web of well-being.

In life, consciously choosing happiness becomes a transformative practice. It invites us to cultivate an internal landscape filled with positivity, gratitude, and joy. By aligning our intentions with the universal flow, we shape a life that transcends mere existence, embracing fulfillment and harmony as essential elements of our journey. The practice of choosing happiness serves as a guiding compass, leading us to a destination where our inner joy harmonizes with the cosmic dance of existence.

***

These principles are not merely the goals of our journey but the vibrant threads that weave together a life rich in meaning and alignment with the cosmic dance. As we continue our journey, may these guiding lights illuminate our path, offering inspiration, resilience, and a profound connection to the intricate flow of the universe. May we navigate life with grace and joy, co-creating a reality that reflects the beauty and abundance inherent in the cosmic dance.

MY PERSONAL MANTRA

"Hi, my name is Sam, and now I'm so HAPPY and feel so GOOD, because of how far I've come in my life and because of all the great things coming my way right now. I'm blessed, appreciative, grateful, and thankful for everything I have, all I had, all the experiences I went through, and everything I'm going through right now. And I know, like I know, like I know with unwavering faith that all this is happening for a reason, a good reason, actually it's a great reason. It's just the universe responding to the nature of my soul, to the song of my heart, and to my prayers. And I know, like I know, like I know with unwavering faith that the universe is rearranging itself for me right now to give me exactly what I want. And what I want is: ...., ..., ..., ..., ... And I know, like I know, like I know with unwavering faith that this is all happening for me right now, and that I'm pulling off a miracle, the miracle of harnessing the flow of the universe. Amen and thank you."

BOOK COVER INSPERATION

In the pursuit of the perfect cover for my book, "Harnessing the Flow of the Universe," I embarked on a visual journey that mirrored the essence of the ideas captured within these pages. The central theme of the book revolves around the profound concept of aligning oneself with the cosmic currents, akin to a maestro conducting the symphony of the universe.

As I delved into the huge stretch of imagery, my search was fueled by a desire to find a visual representation that would not only captivate the reader's attention but also summarize the essence of the book's message. The notion of hands steering the cosmic flow or a silhouette facing the universe like a maestro directing a grand orchestra was at the forefront of my mind.

It was during this quest that I stumbled upon a remarkable image that immediately resonated with the core message of my book. The image, which now graces the cover, is a captivating scene: an astronaut, not tied by the usual constraints of space, skillfully rides a skateboard through the cosmic currents.

The astronaut, surrounded by the celestial wonders of the universe, embodies the harmonious interaction between an individual and the vast cosmic forces. The skateboard becomes a metaphorical vehicle, symbolizing the ability to navigate the patterns of the universe with finesse and control. This visual metaphor captures the essence of harnessing the flow of the universe in a way that is both imaginative and attention-grabbing.

The astronaut's posture displays confidence and mastery, emphasizing the idea that, with understanding and alignment, we can ride the waves of the universe with skill and purpose. The cosmic scenery, with its mesmerizing blend of stars and galaxies, further reinforces the idea of a harmonious dance between the individual and the cosmic energies.

In conclusion, the chosen cover summarizes the very spirit of "Harnessing the Flow of the Universe" – a journey of empowerment, wisdom, and the artful navigation of life's cosmic currents. It is my hope that this visually striking cover not only invites readers but also sparks their curiosity to explore the profound insights within the pages of the book.